Pattern Cutting

Pattern Cutting

Margaret Melliar

B. T. Batsford Ltd London

© Margaret Melliar 1968
First published 1968
ISBN 0 7134 2897 X

Reprinted 1970
Reprinted 1972
Reprinted 1974
Printed in Great Britain by
The Anchor Press Ltd, Tiptree, Essex
for the publishers
B. T. BATSFORD LTD
4 Fitzhardinge Street, London W1

Contents

Foreword

This book has been written in response to the growing demand for more information on the technicalities of Pattern Cutting and as a textbook for students taking the City and Guild's of London Institute examinations in Dressmaking and Dressmanufacture.

The success today of London as a fashion centre is largely due to the influx of recently trained college students into the pattern cutting and design rooms in the wholesale dress industry. With their success, more and more students are training to be fashion designers, and it is with these particular students in mind that this book has been created.

If some sections of the book appear limited in scope, it is because with the amount of space available, it is not possible to delve as deeply or range as widely as I would like into every aspect of cutting. However, the basic principles for cutting all types of garments are illustrated, and will supply students with sufficient knowledge for them to continue investigating and experimenting for themselves.

I am indebted to Miss E S McEwan, my predecessor at Hornsey College of Art, who has kindly permitted me to make use of her method of drafting lingerie, and children's wear. I would also like to thank the Clothing Institute for allowing me to make use of their library facilities; and the British Standards Institution for letting me publish extracts from their Children's Body Measurement Chart. And lastly, but not least, my thanks go to Miss Thelma Nye of Batsfords, who has given me so much encouragement and help in the many intricacies of producing a book of this type.

Reigate 1968   Margaret Melliar

Introduction

Fashion is always changing, but the principles of pattern cutting remain the same, and once learnt, can be applied to the many hundreds of varying styles dictated by fashion.

This book sets out to show how, by using a basic block, patterns can be adapted to any style without the complication of having to draft out each design separately. The method of using and adapting a basic block is extensively used by the wholesale dress trade today—the block pattern being made to fit the sample sized figure. The aspiring young student who wishes to become a fashion designer will therefore be well advised to follow the cutting instructions as laid out in this book page by page to gain a thorough knowledge of the basic principles of cutting; for it is in the pattern cutting room he will commence his career as an assistant cutter, before graduating as a fully fledged dress designer.

Block patterns change very little from season to season; modifications such as length of skirt, padding for shoulders, etc. can be added in accordance with the prevailing fashion. The same basic block is used throughout this book with modifications added for cutting coats and for lingerie. For children's wear, the method of adapting a block pattern for all styles is also employed, but in this case it is necessary to draft out a separate bodice block for each age group.

Pattern cutting is essentially a practical process where an eye for line and proportion is a far greater asset than the ability to work out calculations, for you must remember that in pattern cutting you are fitting the human form and not working out sums. It is assumed that anybody using this book will have a thorough knowledge of dressmaking and students should be conversant with methods of making up before they turn their hand to pattern cutting.

This book is intended to help the young teacher as well as the student and home dressmaker; and it has been planned as a ready reference book where information can be obtained at a glance; each section is carefully graded from the simple to the more complicated. Fashion styles today are basically very simple, but they may easily change again to more complicated styling with seaming and pocket detail; and the student will then be glad of the knowledge attained.

At the date of printing even some of the most contemporary styles in this book may appear outmoded, but the basic principles of cutting will remain; and it is the experience of cutting the many styles shown which will be needed by the designer-cutter if he is to be a good exponent of his craft.

About block patterns

In flat pattern cutting, a foundation or *block pattern* is first made to fit the sample sized figure. The block pattern has no style lines, but it fits the figure snugly, the form being obtained by the introduction of darts at shoulder and waist. The more prominent the bust formation is, the wider the darts should be.

The block pattern is a guide to making the master pattern for new designs. Style lines, pleats, tucks, godets, pockets, etc. are placed on the block according to the style to be cut. From one basic block many styles can be obtained, whilst still retaining the size and fit.

The draft of the bodice block shown here, is based on the Direct Measurement System. Direct measurements are taken of the human figure and applied to the draft. With accurate taking of measurements, this is considered as one of the most effective methods of constructing a block. The block used here has 3 in. ease round the bust, and fits the figure comfortably and the shoulder line follows the natural slope of the shoulders without padding. If shoulder pads are to be used, add 1 to $1\frac{1}{2}$ in. extra height to the shoulder tip. In this block, the shoulder seam is also centralized, enabling the block to be used unaltered when cutting drop shoulders, raglan and kimono sleeves.

The draft given here is for a bodice block fitting bust size 34 in. and hips 37 in. but it can also be drafted successfully to individual measurements; it is advisable, however, in order to be thoroughly conversant with the block, to begin by drafting out the 34 bust size several times before embarking on one to individual measurements.

Students are often of the impression that there is only one method of drafting a *basic block*, but in fact, there are many; and the resulting blocks may vary very slightly. Some blocks may have as much as 4 in. ease round the bust, and this is usually the amount of ease added when drafting blouses—and others may have as little as 2 in. ease; which is the minimum specified by the British Standards Institution. Again, with the current trend for rather skinny fitting tops to bodices, some manufacturers may reduce the quantity of ease even more round the bust. However, whichever method is employed to draft the block, the resulting balance of the blocks should remain the same, i.e. the measurement of the front shoulder to waist should always be at least 1 in. longer than the back measurement of shoulder to waist.

When drafting a block to personal measurements it is advisable to test it out by cutting out and making it up in mull or unbleached calico and trying it on for fit. Mark the centre front with tacking stitches and pin in place, then check to see that both the bust and the hip line are on the straight grain. The neck should fit snugly, and the armhole should be high under the arm. Regarding the waist fitting, no more than $1\frac{1}{2}$ in. should be taken out of the side seam; the rest of the surplus should be taken out in the waist dart.

At this stage one cannot over-emphasise the importance of extreme care in drafting and checking the block pattern. Once the student has ascertained that the block is a perfect fit, she can then proceed with confidence, knowing that all patterns based on that block will fit well. And it makes it possible sometimes to dispense with the second fitting when making up.

The chart of Standard Body Measurements on page 13 will be helpful as a guide and a check when drafting various sized blocks; and it is essential to refer to these when grading blocks to trade sizes. One basic point to be borne in mind is that the shoulder length is always governed by the *across back* measurement; therefore it is essential that in order to obtain a perfect fitting block pattern, body measurements must be taken with the greatest possible accuracy.

Block patterns are always cut without seam allowances. These should be added when cutting out in fabric; $\frac{1}{2}$ in. should be added to all seams except round armhole and neck where only $\frac{1}{4}$ in. seam allowance is necessary. Throughout this book, arrows depict the straight grain of the fabric.

Correct method of taking body measurements

As garment cutting is based on measurements of the figure, it stands to reason that they must be taken with the utmost accuracy. Students should first practise on a dummy dress stand, before taking measurements of the human figure. Continual practice will give proficiency in this direction, and it is helpful for students to work in pairs. When measuring the figure, the person should wear a plain dress or jumper, with a high close neck, and plain set-in sleeves. It is advisable to take the measurements in a set sequence, as set out here; this also being the correct order for construction lines when drafting the bodice block. The back measurements are taken first, then the girth, then the front, and lastly the arms. When taking girth measurements, you should stand on the left-hand side of the person being measured. All girth measurements should be taken tightly, as ease for movement is incorporated in the draft.

Order of taking measurements

1 *Nape of neck to waist back*
2 *Full length*
3 *Length from waist to ground*
4 *Across back*
5 *Bust measurement*
6 *Waist measurement*
7 *Hip measurement*
8 *Across chest*
9 *Shoulder length*
10 *Sleeve length*
11 *Short sleeve length*
12 *Round upper arm*
13 *Round elbow*
14 *Round wrist*

1 *Nape of neck to waist back* Measure from the seventh cervical bone at the back of the neck to the natural back waist line (to locate this, tie a cord tightly round the waist).
2 *Full length* Measure from nape of neck to waist back, then continue to hem of skirt.
3 *Waist to ground* Taken at centre back from natural waist to floor level.
4 *Across back* This should be measured from armhole to armhole, 4 in. down from nape of neck. (This measurement should be ¼ of the total length from back neck to waist.)
5 *Bust measurement* Stand on the left-hand side of the person being measured, and pass the tape-measure round the fullest part of the bust, and slightly higher at the back. If the tape-measure drops at the back, the resulting measurement may be too small.
6 *Waist measurement* This should be taken tightly, as ease will be allowed on the draft.
7 *Hip measurement* This must be taken round the widest part of the hips; 8 in. below the waist. It may be as short as 7 in. on a short person or as deep as 9 in. on a tall figure. Take this measurement tightly.
8 *Across chest* Stand facing the figure and take this measurement 4 in. down from the pit of the neck. Measure from armhole to armhole.
9 *Shoulder length* Measure on top of the shoulder from neck to arm bone.
10 *Sleeve length* Measure from tip of shoulder, round back of elbow to the wrist bone near the little finger.

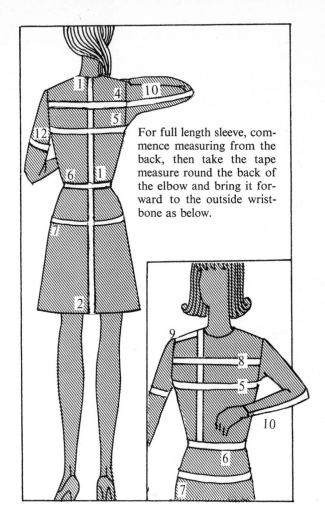

For full length sleeve, commence measuring from the back, then take the tape measure round the back of the elbow and bring it forward to the outside wrist-bone as below.

Note the position of the arm, which should be bent, as shown in the illustration. This measurement is best taken from the back.

11 *Short sleeve length* Should be noted at the same time as measuring the long sleeve. It is usually about 10 in. shorter.
12 *Round upper arm* Taken round fullest part of the arm muscle.
13 *Round elbow* Put the tape-measure in crook of arm and bend arm as much as possible. This will give the smallest measure that would be possible round the sleeve elbow.
14 *Wrist measure* Taken comfortably round the wrist.

The above will be your own personal body measurements. Keep them carefully for drafting out your own *bodice blocks*. These are essential measurements from which to work, and if you have taken them accurately the resulting block should fit well. Before drafting a bodice block to your own measurements, it is recommended that you practice drafting out the sample sized block overleaf. Once you have grasped the procedure of drafting out the block, you will finally be able to draft the bodice block to any set of given measurements.

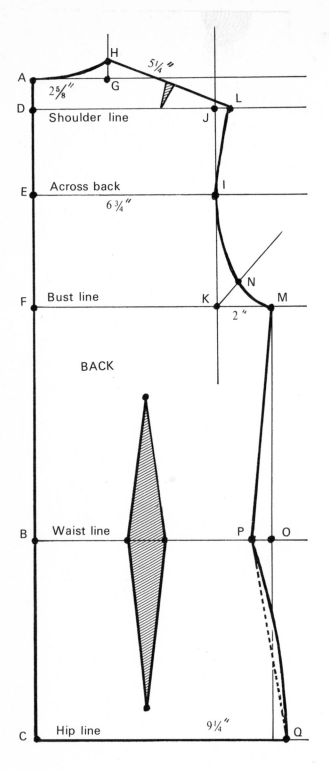

Back bodice draft

Bust size 34 in.
Neck to waist	16 in.	*Hip measure*	37 in.
Neck to hips	24 in.	*Shoulder line*	4¾ in.
Across back	13½ in.	*Armhole*	16½ in.
Bust measure	34 in.		
Waist	26 in.		

1 Rule line A to B. Neck to waist 16 in. (or personal measure). 2 Continue AB to C, 8 in. below waist level = 24 in. Square out for *hip line*. 3 At point A square out for *back neck line*, then square out the following construction lines:

Point D is 1 in. from A, square out for *shoulder line*.

Point E is 4 in. from A, square out for the *across back line*. The position of this is estimated as being ¼ of the back length from neck to waist.

Point F is 8 in. from A, square out for *bust line*. This is estimated as being halfway between neck and waist.

Point B is 16 in. from A, and is the neck to waist length. Square out for *waist line*.

Point C is 8 in. below the waist, square out here for the *hip line*. All these lines should be drawn at right angles to line AC and are *construction lines*. 4 To construct *back neck*, measure 2⅝ in. along neck line to G. The neck width is calculated as being 1/12th of the bust measure, minus ¼ in. At G measure up ⅝ in. to point H. Join A to H with a curved line forming half the back neck. 5 On *across back* line, measure half the across back measurement; in this size 6¾ in. and mark this point I. This is an important measurement, as both the width of the shoulder and the placement of the side seam are constructed from this. 6 Square up and down from I and when the line crosses the shoulder line mark this J and where it crosses the bust line mark this K. 7 At J measure out ½ in. to L. Join L to H forming the shoulder slope. (This will actually measure 5 in. but ¼ in. is taken out in a small dart in the centre of the back shoulder line; this helps to fit the bodice back nicely over the curve of the shoulder blade.) 8 To construct the *armhole*, join L to I with a curve. To complete the armhole, extend the *bust line* 2 in. from K to M, then rule a diagonal line through K at 45°. Measure along this line 1¼ in. to N. Join I-N-M completing the armhole. 9 To obtain the *side seam*, square down from M crossing over waist line at O to hip level. For semi-fitted waist, measure in ¾ in. from O to P. No more than this should be taken out of the side seam—the remainder of the waist suppression will be taken out of the waist dart. Join P to M with a straight line. 10 For *hip width*, measure ¼ hip measurement along the hip line to Q. Join P to Q. This line may be slightly curved in a convex line for hip formation. 11 The *waist dart* is best located by fitting the back on the human figure or dress stand and the surplus taken-in as a dart placed midway between B and P. In this draft, the dart is 1½ in. wide, and extends 5 in. above the waist line, and 6 in. below.

Note that no ease is allowed on the *back* draft; all ease should be added to the *front block*.

Note

In all sizes other than bust 34 in., make line FM ¼ bust measurement. The neck widens at H ⅛ in. per 2 in. size increase, and narrows ⅛ in. per size decrease.

Front bodice draft

Bust size 34 in.

The front bodice draft is constructed on the back bodice. The dotted lines indicate the outline of the back block. A shoulder dart has to be added to the front bodice, to give it form; and the extra length taken up by the bust prominence is added by dropping the waist line ¾ in. at centre front, graduating to nothing at the side seam. The amount taken out by the shoulder dart is added on to the armhole; and ease for movement is added on to the side seams.

1 Re-draft the back bodice. 2 Neck drops 1¾ in. in C front to B. Join C to B with a curve. 3 To obtain *shoulder dart*, measure 4 in. in from centre front along bust line to D, then drop down 1 in. to E. This is the bust point. In larger sizes, this will move outwards from centre front ¼ in. for every 2 in. increase in bust measure. 4 Along *shoulder slope*, locate F 2¼ in. from C. Rule a line from bust point through D to F. 5 For *width of dart*, the amount taken out for the dart width should equal the amount taken out for the neck width; in this case, 2½ in. Measure along shoulder slope 2½ in. from F to G. 6 Complete *shoulder dart* by joining E to G. 7 To construct the *shoulder point*, extend the shoulder slope and locate point H which should be the same distance from G as point F. 8 To construct the *arm-hole*, extend the across back line to point K. J to K should equal the amount taken out by the shoulder dart on the cross back line. Point M is ¼ in. forward on the diagonal line from L. At N extend the bust line 1½ in. to O. This is the total *ease* allowance. 9 Complete *armhole* by connecting H, K, M and O with a curved line. It is important that the curve drops a little below the bust line between N and O. 10 For *side seam* add 1 in. ease allowance at waist level. Mark this point Q, also add 1 in. ease on the hip line at R. Call this point S. Join O, Q, S to form the side seam. The line from Q to S over the hip may be slightly curved if so desired. 11 To obtain correct *dart shaping* on the shoulder slope, first drop ¼ in. from H to I, then cut out the bodice front, leaving the shoulder slope uncut. Pin in the dart with the fold towards the neck, then lay a ruler along the shoulder slope and across the fold and rule a line from the shoulder point I to the neck point C. Cut along this line with the dart folded, then open. This will give you the correct dart shaping. 12 For *front waist line*, measure ¾ in. from T to U and draw in the new waist line with a curved line graduating to nothing at Q. The total front length from base of neck to C front waist should now measure 15 in. 13 The front *waist dart*, as in the back, is best located by fitting the bodice on a 34 bust size dress stand and taking in the surplus to form a dart. For placement of dart, the centre of the dart should be 1½ in. to the outside of the bust point. In this draft, make the waist dart 1½ in. wide and extend 5 in. above the waist, and 6 in. below the waist as illustrated.

Now check your pattern. The total armhole should

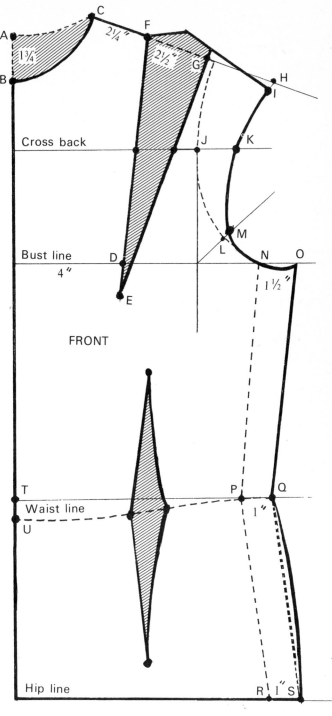

measure 16½ in., the neck should measure 13⅞ in. and the shoulder length 4¾ in.

Ease allowance The total allowance for *ease* which is added on to the *front block* only is 3 in. on the bust, 2 in. at waist level, and 2 in. on the hips. Thus actual *garment measures* of the block are bust 37 in., waist 28 in., and hips 39 in.

The bodice block

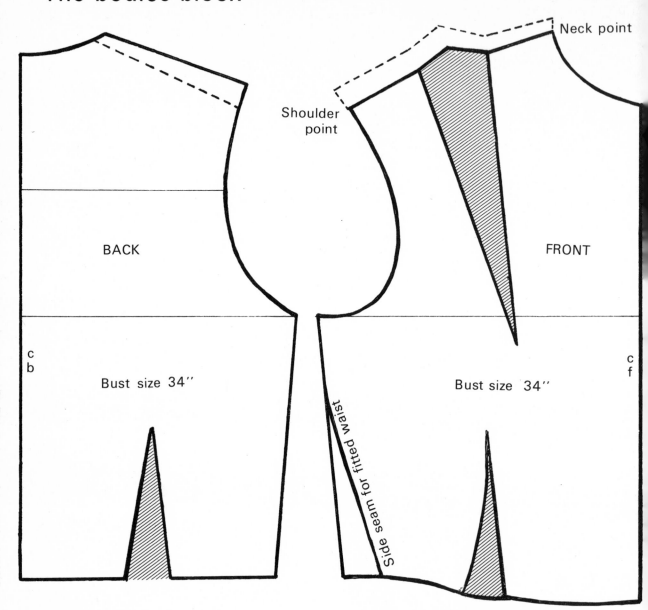

Neck point

Shoulder point

BACK

FRONT

c b

c f

Bust size 34″

Bust size 34″

Side seam for fitted waist

Solid outline block

The solid outline shows the bodice blocks cut down to waist level. In order to follow the exercises set out on manipulating the bust and waist darts, it will be necessary to cut the blocks to waist level as illustrated. This block is drafted with the centralized shoulder seam commonly used in the wholesale trade, and always used for cutting styles with *Raglan*, *Dolman*, and sleeves cut in one piece or as part of the bodice. For convenience the block with the centralized shoulder seam is used throughout this book.

Block with dotted shoulder line

The dotted shoulder line shows the block as it is sometimes used for styles with set-in sleeves and frequently used by the retail dress trade. This gives a shoulder seam that slopes more towards the back, and is obtained by removing a strip from off the back shoulder and placing it on to the front shoulder as illustrated. The amount cut from the back is $\frac{3}{8}$ in. at the neck point and $\frac{3}{4}$ in. at the shoulder tip. This block with its more sloping shoulder seam is helpful in making the shoulders appear narrower. For a tightly fitted waist, the side seam can be taken in an inch as illustrated.

Standard body measurements

List of average measurements (*in inches*)

1 Bust	30	32	34	36	38	40	42	44	46
2 Waist	22	24	26	28	30	32	34	36	38
3 Hips	33	35	37	39	41	43	45	47	49
4 Across back	$12\frac{1}{2}$	13	$13\frac{1}{2}$	14	$14\frac{1}{2}$	15	$15\frac{1}{2}$	$15\frac{3}{4}$	16
5 Across chest	$13\frac{1}{2}$	14	$14\frac{1}{2}$	15	$15\frac{1}{2}$	16	$16\frac{1}{2}$	$16\frac{3}{4}$	17
6 Shoulder length	$4\frac{1}{4}$	$4\frac{1}{2}$	$4\frac{3}{4}$	5	$5\frac{1}{4}$	$5\frac{1}{4}$	$5\frac{3}{8}$	$5\frac{1}{2}$	$5\frac{5}{8}$
7 Length from waist to neck at CB	$14\frac{3}{4}$	15	$15\frac{1}{4}$	$15\frac{1}{2}$	$15\frac{3}{4}$	16	$16\frac{1}{4}$	$16\frac{1}{2}$	$16\frac{3}{4}$
8 Length from waist to ground	*no average—too variable*								
9 Length from shoulder to wrist	$21\frac{1}{2}$	22	$22\frac{1}{2}$	23	$23\frac{1}{2}$	24	$24\frac{1}{2}$	to	25
10 Length from shoulder to elbow	$11\frac{1}{2}$	12	$12\frac{1}{2}$	13	$13\frac{1}{2}$	14	14	to	15
11 Round upper arm	$10\frac{1}{2}$	11	$11\frac{1}{2}$	12	$12\frac{1}{2}$	13	$13\frac{1}{2}$	to	15
12 Round elbow	$10\frac{1}{2}$	11	$11\frac{1}{2}$	12	$12\frac{1}{2}$	13	$13\frac{1}{2}$	to	15
13 Round wrist	$5\frac{3}{4}$	6	$6\frac{1}{4}$	$6\frac{1}{2}$	$6\frac{3}{4}$	7	$7\frac{1}{4}$	to	$7\frac{1}{2}$
14 Length from neck to armhole	$7\frac{3}{4}$	8	$8\frac{1}{4}$	$8\frac{1}{2}$	$8\frac{1}{2}$	$8\frac{3}{4}$	9	$9\frac{1}{4}$	$9\frac{1}{2}$
15 Neck width	$2\frac{1}{8}$	$2\frac{1}{4}$	$2\frac{3}{8}$	$2\frac{1}{2}$	$2\frac{5}{8}$	$2\frac{3}{4}$	$2\frac{7}{8}$	3	3
16 Width for shoulder slope	6	6	$6\frac{1}{4}$	$6\frac{1}{4}$	$6\frac{3}{8}$	$6\frac{1}{2}$	$6\frac{5}{8}$	$6\frac{3}{4}$	$6\frac{7}{8}$
17 Bust width	$3\frac{3}{4}$	$3\frac{3}{4}$	$3\frac{7}{8}$	4	$4\frac{1}{4}$	$4\frac{1}{4}$	$4\frac{3}{4}$	$4\frac{1}{2}$	$4\frac{5}{8}$
18 Dart width	$2\frac{1}{4}$	$2\frac{1}{2}$	$2\frac{3}{4}$	3	$3\frac{1}{4}$	$3\frac{1}{2}$	$3\frac{3}{4}$	4	$4\frac{1}{4}$
19 Armhole	$15\frac{1}{2}$	16	$16\frac{1}{2}$	17	$17\frac{1}{2}$	18	$18\frac{1}{2}$	19	20
20 Depth of crown	$4\frac{3}{8}$	$4\frac{3}{4}$	$4\frac{7}{8}$	5	$5\frac{1}{8}$	$5\frac{1}{4}$	$5\frac{3}{8}$	$5\frac{1}{2}$	$5\frac{3}{4}$

Other types of bodice blocks

The normal bodice block has 2 darts; one in the shoulder seam for bust fitting, and the other at the waist for waist suppression. Both these darts can be moved according to the style of the garment and seam placement and with the present fashion of semi-fitted, easy fitting clothes, the waist dart is often ignored. The shoulder dart however must be incorporated somewhere into the bodice if the garment is to have the correct balance. For certain styles it is best not to have a shoulder dart; the illustrations here show how it can be shifted to other parts of the bodice. It is a good plan to cut a set of blocks as shown in B, C, D, E and F.

1 To obtain block B as shown in fig. 1, draw round your original front block marking in the shoulder and waist darts. Measure 2 in. down from the armhole and rule a dotted line to the point of the shoulder dart. Cut out the bodice, and cut along the dotted line. Then pin in the shoulder dart. This transfers the shoulder dart to under the arm; but it must be shortened to about 3 in. in length. Pin on to fresh paper, and re-draw for new

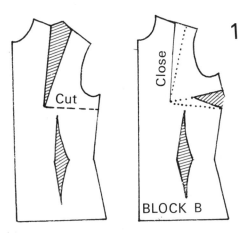

Cut
Close
BLOCK B
1

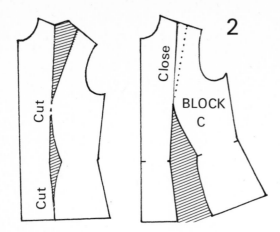

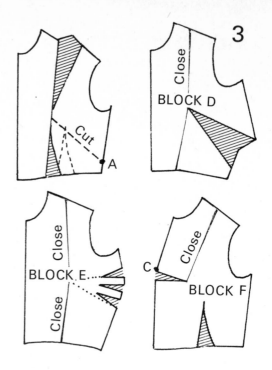

block. 2 Block C is used for fitted styles, and is used when features such as draping or pocket detail spring from the dart. Draw round the original block; and move the waist dart to line up immediately below the bust dart. To do this, lay a ruler along the inner line of the bust dart, and extend it to the waist. This gives the positioning for the waist dart. Cut out the bodice, then cut from the hem up to the point of the bust dart along the dotted line as illustrated, and pin in the shoulder dart. This causes the shoulder dart fullness to be transferred into a very large waist dart as shown in block C. As can be seen, this causes the side body part of the bodice to be thrown on to the *bias* grain of the fabric giving a close fit to the figure. 3 Blocks D, E and F can only be obtained by cutting the block through at waist level. In block D the diagonal dart is known as a *French dart*, and is obtained by folding both shoulder and waist darts to meet at the bust point then cutting from A along the dotted line to the bust point. The result will be a very large dart as shown in block D. This is often

used in a decorative way, and made the design feature of the garment. Both blocks E and F have their uses. To obtain block E, transfer both shoulder and waist dart fullness to under the arm. It is unsightly to have one big dart in this placement, so it should be divided into 3 smaller darts as illustrated. In block F the shoulder dart is shifted to the centre front of the bodice. Mark point C 7 in. down from the neck, and cut to the point of the bust dart. Close shoulder dart, transferring the fullness to the centre front. This is useful for certain styles.

Disproportion and the basic block

The bodice block when drafted will fit the figure of average proportions, but the construction of the human form follows various figure types, and there are many people whose proportions are slightly away from the average, for these, the bodice block of the appropriate size can be adapted to fit as follows.

1 Long back balance

If a dress prepared from a normal pattern is fitted on a *round shouldered* figure, you will get the effect illustrated in fig. 1. It will be tight across the hips in front, and hang away at the back; it will also be too short in length at the back. This type of figure requires what is known as *long back balance*, and this is achieved by increasing the

distance from A to B. Slash through the block on the across back line and open the required amount as shown. The centre back line will now be rounded instead of straight, which is exactly what this figure requires. At the same time, it will usually be necessary to cut the back without a centre seam; one method of doing this is shown in fig. 1B. This shows the lower part of the back placed against the fold edge of the material; a space is now left at the top of the back neck. This quantity represents the exact amount of disproportion, and it may be eliminated by taking out 2 or 3 vertical tucks in the back neck. The quantity taken out by the tucks should equal the distance between A and C.

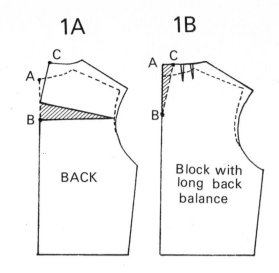

2 Long front balance

This is found in the figure of very upright carriage and usually associated with abnormal bust development. If a normal frock is fitted on this type of figure, it will show the defects illustrated in fig. 2B. It will be tight across the hips at the back, and will hang away from the figure in front; it will also be shorter in front than at the back. This indicates that the pattern is too short in *front balance* and is rectified as follows. The pattern is cut across the front from 1 to 2 and opened out to the required extent between 1 and 3. In actually cutting from material, with the centre front to the fold, the surplus between 4 and 5 must be dealt with in exactly the same way as it was at the back. Instead of introducing pin tucks, the bust dart must be increased. Should the dress have a V neck, this amount may be ignored unless the amount of disproportion is very large.

3 Excessive bust development

Another common form of disproportion is that of excessive bust development in comparison with shoulder size. This is corrected by splitting the pattern in front through from top to bottom, and opening it out to the required extent and making the bust dart larger as shown. This is usually found in conjunction with long front balance. Whilst this kind of disproportion is found mostly in larger sizes, a similar variety is sometimes encountered in very small ones—a woman with a 32 in. or 33 in. bust will sometimes possess a very fully formed figure together with a small waist. This can best be dealt with by splitting the pattern down to the waist and opening it in the top section only, leaving the waist size unaltered; this method of increasing the size of the shoulder dart will greatly increase the bust formation.

Bear in mind always that it is the function of the designer and cutter to disguise disproportion as far as possible by artistic draping, and to avoid making it more obvious by too close a fit.

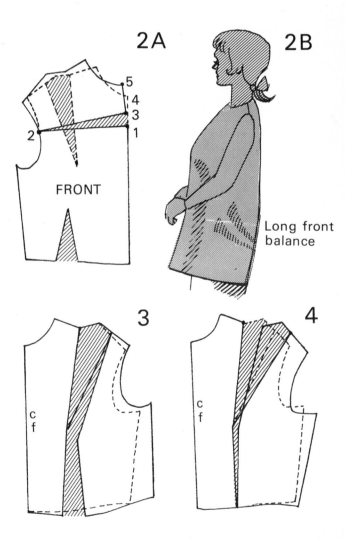

Manipulation of the bodice darts

You have now learned how to draft a block pattern in which the essential form is produced by means of a dart from shoulder to bust point, and waist to bust. The bust dart being merely a mechanical aid to fit, should be dispensed with where possible; and through block manipulation it is possible to shift the shoulder dart into another part of the bodice, whilst still retaining the essential form. The following diagrams show how you can move the darts; also how they can be incorporated into a style seam.

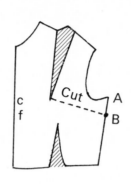
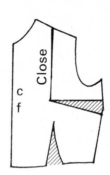
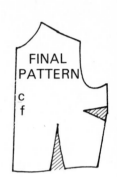

Style 1 1 Take your bodice block and draw round it in pencil, marking in clearly both darts. Measure 2 in. down from A to B and rule a line to the bust point. 2 Cut out bodice. 3 Cut along the dotted line to bust point; then close the shoulder dart. The fullness is now transferred to under the arm. 4 Shorten the underarm dart, making it 2½-3 in. long. Re-draw on fresh paper for final pattern.

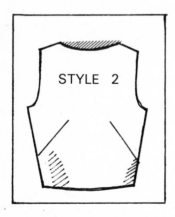
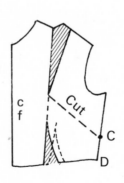
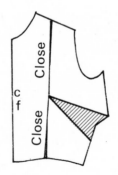
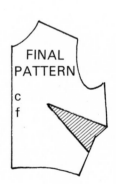

Style 2 This bodice shows a semi-fitted waist with no dart. Both bust and waist darts are transferred into the diagonal French dart. 1 Mark point C 2 in. up from D, then rule a dotted line from C to bust point. 2 Cut out bodice, and cut along dotted line from C up to bust point. 3 Move waist dart forward to line up with bust point. 4 Pin in both darts, and re-draw on fresh paper for final pattern.

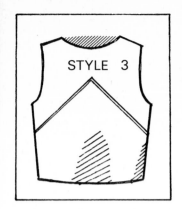

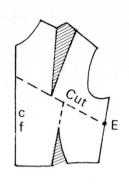

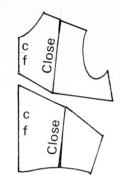

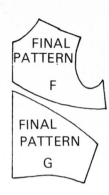

Style 3 In this style, both darts are incorporated into a style seam forming a yoke. 1 Mark E 2 in. below armhole. Draw a line from E passing through the bust point to centre front. 2 Extend waist dart to dotted line. 3

Cut out bodice, then cut along the dotted line forming the pattern into 2 sections, F and G. The dart fitting is now transferred into the style seam. Re-draw for final pattern.

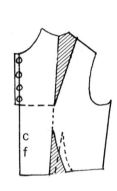

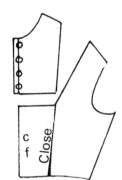

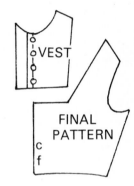

Style 4 1 Draw round bodice block adding ¾ in. button extension, marking in the darts, moving the waist dart to immediately under the bust point. Rule a dotted line from bust point horizontally to centre front. 2 Cut along inner line of bust dart and along dotted line to

bust point making vest separate from bodice front. Extend waist dart to bust point and close. Cut away remainder of shoulder dart. 3 Trace round pattern pieces on another sheet of paper. Add 2 in. wide facing up centre front of vest. Cut out for final pattern.

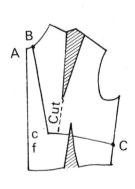

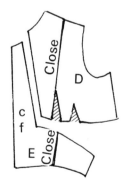

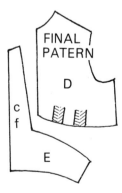

Style 5 1 Draw round bodice block putting in style lines as indicated making B 1 in. from A and C, 2 in. up from waist. 2 Cut out along style lines, forming pattern pieces D and E. Close shoulder dart and cut up dotted line to bust point. Close waist dart in section E. 3 Trace

round pieces D and E on another sheet of paper for final pattern. The two darts in section D can be turned into 2 small pleats each 1 in. wide as indicated. This pattern will now be semi-fitted at the waist without a dart which is now transferred into the style seam.

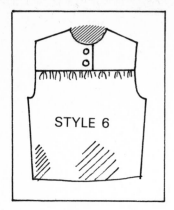

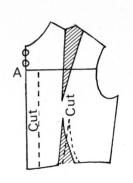

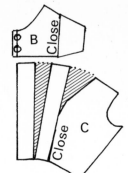

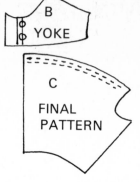

STYLE 6

A

Cut Cut

B Close

B YOKE

C FINAL PATTERN

Close C

Style 6 The diagram here shows how to slash and pivot your block pattern to give greater fullness than can be obtained by transferring the dart. 1 Trace round your bodice block and draw in the yoke and dotted line as indicated, making A 2 in. from pit of neck, and move waist dart to immediately underneath the bust point. 2 Cut along yoke lines forming 2 pattern pieces B and C. Close shoulder dart in B. Cut along dotted lines in C from yoke to waist and pivot out about 4–5 in. for extra fullness. Close waist dart and cut down from bust point to top of waist dart. 3 Pin down on fresh paper and re-draw for final pattern. Add 2 in. wide facing to centre front yoke. The yoke line of section C will now be long enough to gather in the top yoke B as illustrated.

These patterns are cut net with no seam allowance. A $\frac{1}{2}$ in. wide seam allowance must be added to all seams when cutting out in fabric.

Three styles obtained by using the block with underarm dart

These three styles incorporate gathers springing from a shoulder yoke.

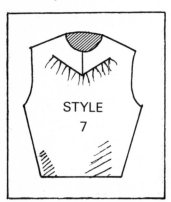

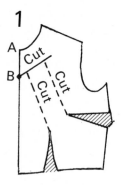

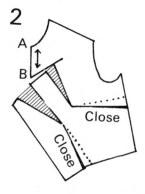

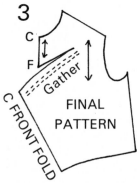

STYLE 7

1

A
B
Cut
Cut
Cut

2

A
B
Close
Close

3

C
F
Gather
C FRONT FOLD
FINAL PATTERN

Style 7 1 Using the block with underarm dart, draw round, marking in yoke line and making B 3 in. from A. 2 Draw dotted lines from points of darts to yoke as illustrated. 3 Cut out bodice and cut from B along yoke line. 4 Fold in darts and cut down dotted lines from yoke to dart points. 5 Lay over fresh paper and re-draw for final pattern. The dart fullness is now transferred into the style seam for gathering or pleating.

When cutting out, lay pattern with yoke CF seam on the straight grain.

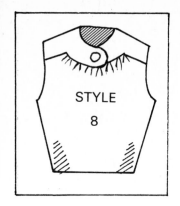
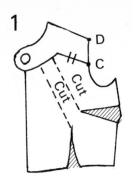
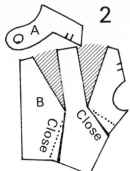
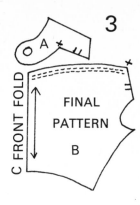

Style 8 1 Draw round block with underarm dart. 2 Draw in shoulder yoke, making C 3 in. down from D. 3 Draw dotted lines to points of darts as illustrated. 4 Cut out, and separate yoke from bodice. Mark these A and B. 5 Cut down dotted lines in section B to points of darts, then fold in the darts. 6 Place over fresh paper and re-draw for final pattern.

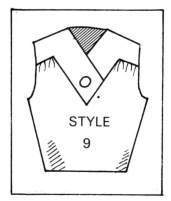
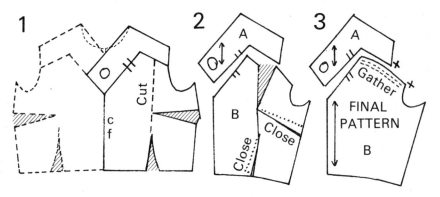

Style 9 1 Lay front blocks together, joining up centre front line and draw round. 2 Draw in shoulder yoke and cross-over front making the V neck cross over 1 in. below pit of neck. 3 Draw dotted line from point of waist dart up to style line. 4 Lengthen underarm dart to touch dotted line as illustrated. 5 Cut out separating yoke section A from bodice section B. 6 Slash down dotted line to point of waist dart, then fold in the darts. This should give sufficient fullness to gather into the yoke. 7 Lay over fresh paper and re-draw for final pattern.

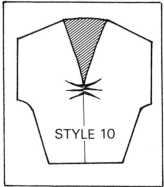

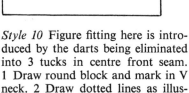
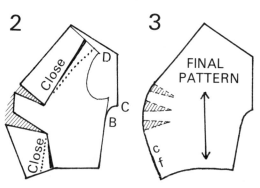

Style 10 Figure fitting here is introduced by the darts being eliminated into 3 tucks in centre front seam. 1 Draw round block and mark in V neck. 2 Draw dotted lines as illustrated from centre front to points of darts. 3 Cut out, then slash along dotted lines from centre front to points of darts. 4 Close darts, bringing extra length to the centre front seam which can be taken in as 3 little pleats. 5 Add cap sleeve by raising shoulder point 1 in. and lower arm 1½ in. Then widen 1 in. to C and draw vertical line up to shoulder.

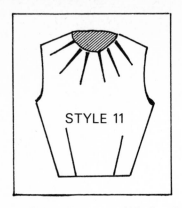

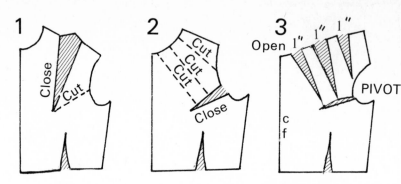

Style 11 1 Draw round block and put in dotted line as illustrated. 2 Cut out, then cut along dotted line from armhole to dart point. 3 Close shoulder dart, transferring dart to armhole. 4 Draw in folds from neck as dotted lines radiating to dart and armhole. 5 Slash along dotted lines from neck, and pivot pattern as illustrated opening each slash 1 in. 6 Lay over fresh paper and re-draw without any dart at the armhole.

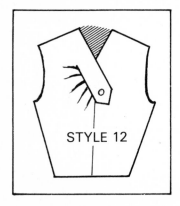

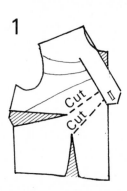

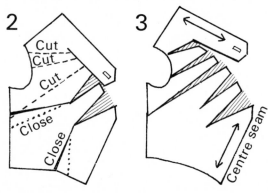

Style 12 In this style, the cutting for the drapery must be done in two stages. 1 Draw round block putting in tab and drapery, making the 2 lower folds terminate at the dart points. 2 Cut out, then cut along lower edge of tab and slash along dotted lines to darts. 3 Close darts, then slash down other fold lines to side seam and armhole as indicated and open required amount for draping. 4 Lay over fresh paper and re-draw for final pattern. The centre front seam must be placed on the straight grain of the fabric; the drapery will then be on the bias.

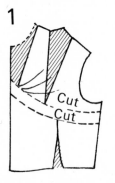

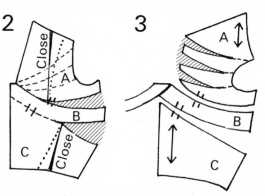

Style 13 This style has a band between upper and lower bodice which is extended for looping as a bow. 1 Draw round block putting in V neck and style features. 2 Cut out band, forming bodice into 3 sections A, B, C. 3 Close shoulder dart and waist dart in sections A and C. 4 Redraw section C on fresh paper. 5 Draw folds in section A as dotted lines from neck to armhole as illustrated. 6 Slash along dotted lines and open each slash about 2 in. for drapery. 7 Lay over fresh paper and re-draw. The arrow must be placed on the straight grain.

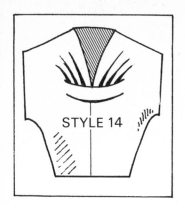

STYLE 14

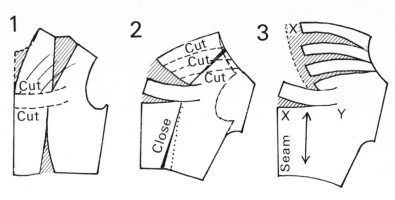

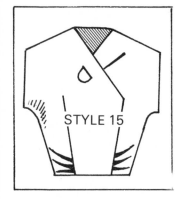

STYLE 15

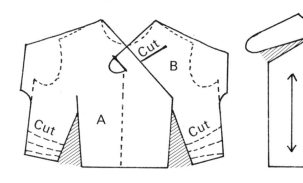

Style 14 In this style, the band hides the seam joining the drapery to the lower bodice; it has to be faced. 1 Draw round block and put in style lines. 2 Cut out, then cut along band lines as illustrated and close darts. 3 Draw in folds as dotted lines extending from top of band to shoulder line as illustrated. 4 Slash along dotted lines from band up to shoulder and open each slash 2–3 in. for the folds. 5 Add 1 in. extra length at X, following the curve of the drapery as shown. This will be joined to line XY when making up.

Style 15 In this style, the tab must be faced, and an opening has to be made in section A for the tab to pass through. 1 Lay bodice fronts together joining up centre front, and draw round. 2 Draw in neck line and tab as illustrated, and mark in drapery folds. 3 Trace through sections A and B separately, and cut out. 4 Slash along dotted fold lines, and open each about 1 in. for draping as illustrated. 5 Cut along lower edge of tab to shoulder in section B and open about 2 in. This will allow space for seam allowance. When the tab is closed, it will form a soft fold.

Three basic jerkins

These three jerkins are all variations of the basic bodice block and are easy to cut as a first exercise for making up in fabric.

1 Draw round block with underarm dart, widen neck 1 in. at A. Add 1 in. button extension down centre front, and fold back paper along extension to give a facing 3 in. wide. Mark point C 7 in. down centre front and cut out V neck with facing still folded, then open out to obtain facing as shown. This style is only semi-fitted, so rule a straight seam from underarm to hip level. Ignore the underarm dart, but the waist dart is used for semi-fitting. Lower and widen the armhole 1 in. all round.

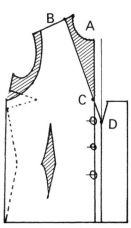

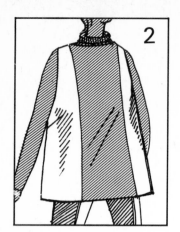

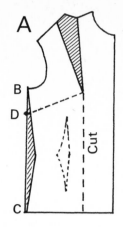

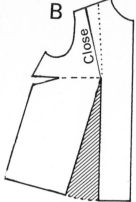

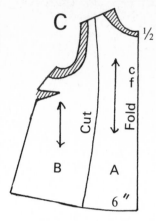

2 This smock has a boat shaped neck line; it is slightly flared, and the centre front panel may be cut in a different coloured material. Rule a line from B to C to straighten the side seam, and draw a dotted line from the hem up to the point of the shoulder dart. Ignore the waist dart. As this pattern has a small dart under the arm, rule a dotted line from D to bust point. Cut along

dotted line to bust point, then fold in shoulder dart transferring the fullness to both underarm dart and hem of smock. Pivot side section to give about 2 in. for underarm dart and then re-draw on fresh paper. Take 1½ in. away from armhole and neck line as illustrated. Then draw a panel seam from centre of shoulder to hem forming the bodice front into sections A and B.

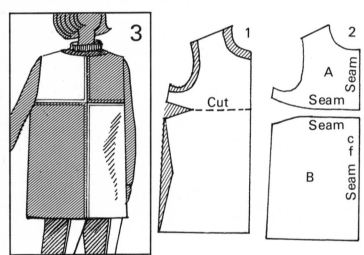

3 A basically simple smock with centre front seam, and the shoulder dart transferred into the yoke seam. This is effective made up in 2 colours. Draw round bodice block with underarm dart. Widen neck 1 in. all round and take 1 in. off all round the armhole. Straighten side seam as illustrated, then cut away underarm dart and along dotted line to centre front to form sections A and B. This can be cut with a centre front seam, and if two colours are used and joined together as illustrated, forms an attractive *tabard* that can be worn with jeans.

Two shirts with knife pleats

Style A This shirt has 3 knife pleats running from shoulder to hem. The pleats are obtained by first pleating the paper, and then laying the bodice block over the pleats, taking care that they are correctly placed. The pattern is then cut out with the pleats closed to ensure correct shaping of pleat openings. 1 First measure in 2 in. from centre front of paper and rule a vertical line parallel to the edge. This will be the facing of the button wrap. 2 Rule 7 more lines 1½ in. apart. 3 Pleat paper

along lines 3, 5 and 7. 4 Crease firmly and lay the bodice block on top, placing the centre front centrally between lines 1 and 2. 5 Draw firmly round the block, then mark buttons down centre front and rule a line ¾ in. inside centre front line for buttonwrap. This should fall on line 2 of the pleated paper. 6 Cut out pattern with pleats folded. 7 Open out pleats and shade in the pleating areas as in diagram.

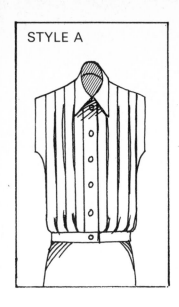

STYLE A

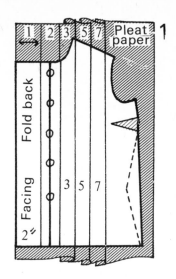

STYLE B

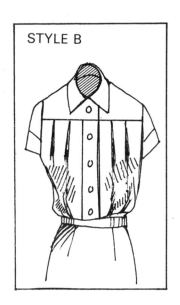

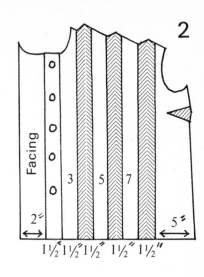

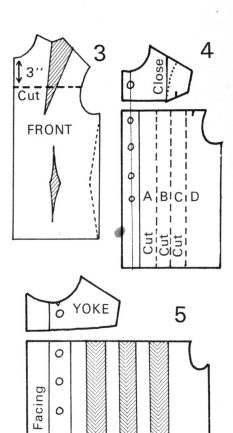

Alternative method of cutting

Style B As an alternative to pleating the paper, this pattern is based on the principle of cutting along the pleat lines and spreading open the required amount for pleating. 1 Draw round the bodice block. 2 Mark in yoke 3 in. down from neck. 4 Cut off yoke, and close shoulder dart. Add ¾ in. button extension down centre front. 5 On remaining bodice, ignore darts and draw in button extension ¾ in. down centre front. 6 Place buttons on centre front line. 7 Draw in pleat lines each 1½ in. apart. Mark spaces between lines A, B, C, D as illustrated. 8 Cut up pleat lines, and spread open each pleat 1½ in. Shade these in as illustrated. 9 Add 2 in. wide facing to yoke, and down blouse front.

French fitted bodice

The French fitted bodice is used predominantly in close fitted bodices. The dart fitting takes the form of 4 long seams running from shoulder to hip line, dividing the bodice into 6 separate pieces. Notching the seams in various places is important for correct joining of pattern pieces. This can be used as a dress block and it is a good idea to cut it out in mull, make it up and try it on.

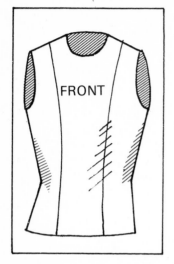

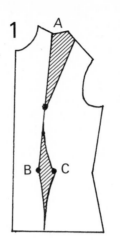

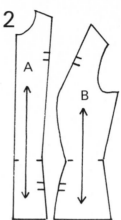

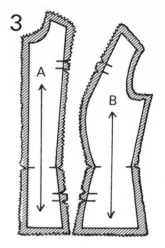

Front bodice 1 The waist dart must be moved to under the shoulder dart; obtain this by laying a ruler along the neck edge of the shoulder dart and continue this to the waist forming a straight line from A to B. Draw in the waist dart and continue to hip level. You can see that the side body section is now very shaped. 2 Cut away side body piece forming sections A and B. Put in balance marks on seams for correct joining.

Back bodice 3 Lay front patterns, just cut, against the shoulder line of the back, matching armholes and neck. The ¼ in. gap in centre of the shoulder forms back dart;

continue this to D on across back line. 4 Continue dart to waist with straight line as in front bodice. Point E is back dart width. Continue E to D with a curved line. Extend waist dart to hip line, then cut out back in 2 sections F and G.

Making up Cut both front and back bodices in mull allowing ⅜ in. seam allowance. Join on all seams matching notches, and join shoulder seam last. Both bust and hip line should be on the straight grain of the fabric. Mark centre front line with blue tacking stitches and try on. Extra fitting can be taken in on the seams if necessary.

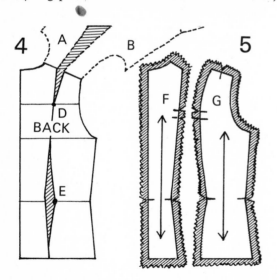

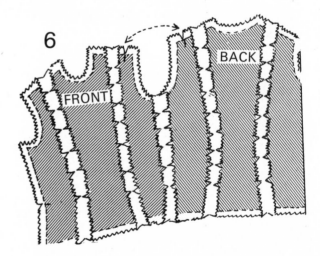

Two styles based on the french fitted bodice

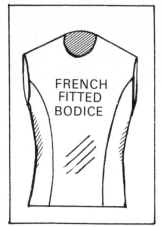

FRENCH FITTED BODICE

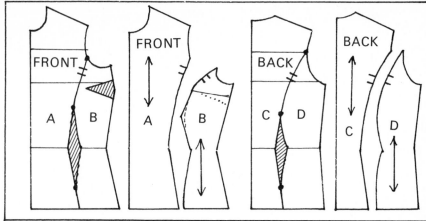

A All dart fullness is transferred to the waist dart.
1 Draw in lines of drapery, and cross-over front. 2 Cut out bodice, then cut along fold lines to side seam and swing each open about 1 in. 3 Re-draw on fresh paper.
B Use block with underarm dart.
1 Lay bodice blocks together joining up centre front.

2 Draw in neck line and double breasted front and pocket. 3 Draw in drapery folds and move waist dart to 2½ in. from centre front and transfer underarm dart into armhole. 4 Trace through section B and cut out. 5 Cut along fold lines from inner to outer edge and swing each open 2 in.

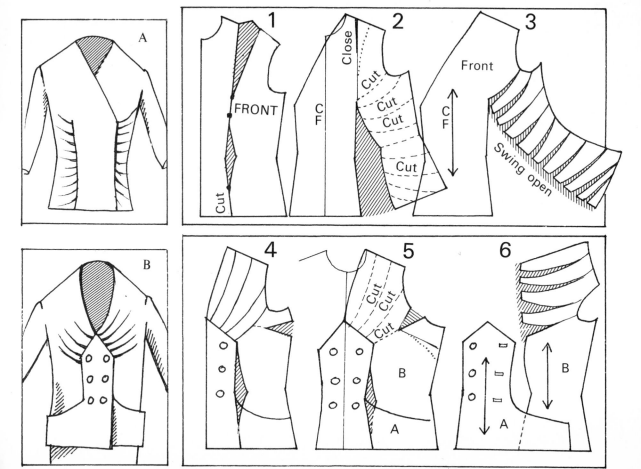

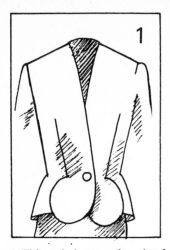
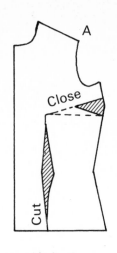
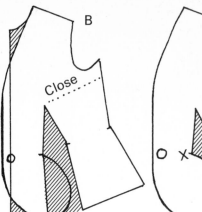
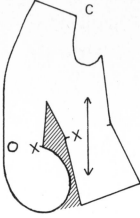

1 This style has novel pocket feature at hip level.
1 Cut up waist dart to the extended point of underarm dart. 2 Close underarm dart, transferring dart to waist. This allows room for the pocket feature to be added. 3 Draw pocket as illustrated. When the waist dart is closed a pocket is formed.

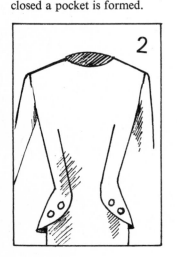
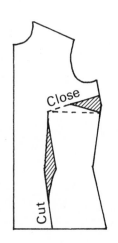
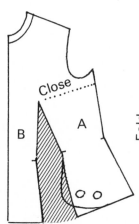
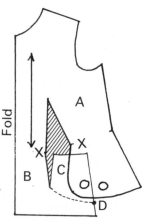

2 There is no seam at the waist of this dress with peplum features; therefore section C must be cut and joined separately—the seam is hidden when the dart is closed.
1 Transfer underarm dart into waist dart. 2 Draw peplum shape on to section A, putting in buttons. 3 To obtain section C, relay bodice block over pattern, and re-draw top of skirt section. 4 Draw a curved line from point of waist dart to D forming section C. This must be traced off and cut separately.
3 Treat this exercise in the same method as A and B. The small pocket forming an integral continuation of the seam is inserted in the space formed by the enlarged waist dart.

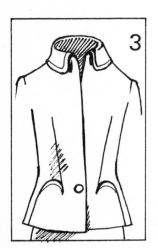
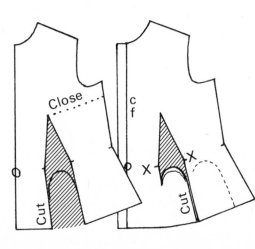

Three styles
with peplums

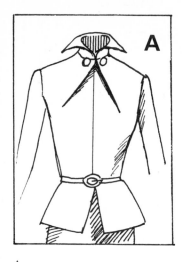

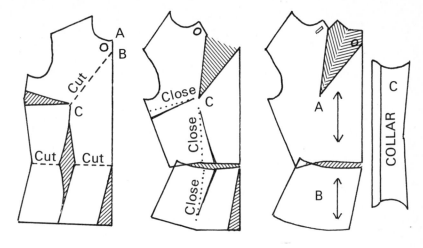

A
1 Draw in style lines. 2 Make A to B 1½ in. and mark dotted line to C. 3 Cut out, then cut along waist line and close the waist dart forming curved peplum. 4 Transfer both darts into the neck by slashing along line BC and closing darts. Place over fresh paper and re-draw bodice and peplum sections A and B. The large dart forms a style feature with the collar.

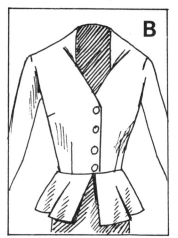

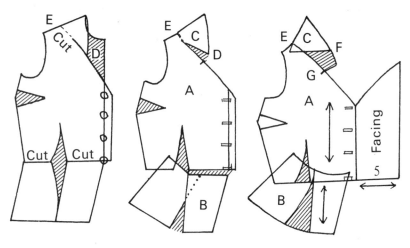

B
1 Draw style lines and add ¾ in. button extension. 2 Cut out, then cut along waist line forming patterns A and B. 3 Flare peplum by cutting through dart in B and overlapping at waist. Re-draw peplum. 4 Slash from D to E separating C. 5 Place section C overlapping at E to form wide dart. Lay over fresh paper and re-draw sections A and B. When F is joined to G it forms the neck line drape.

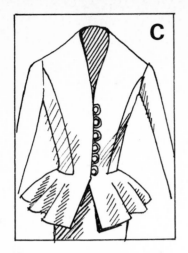

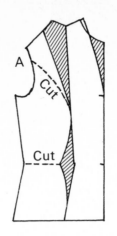

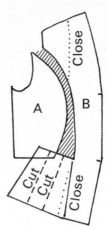

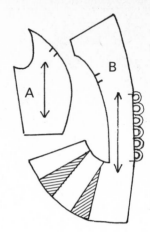

C

1 Draw in style lines making A $2\frac{1}{2}$ in. down from shoulder. 2 Cut along waist to dart and cut away side body piece by cutting up to A. 3 Close dart in B. 4 Close waist dart and flare peplum by cutting and opening the hem in two places. Lay section B over fresh paper and re-draw for final pattern.

Three styles with tab fastening

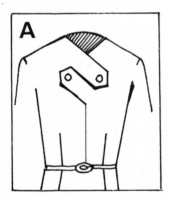

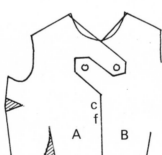

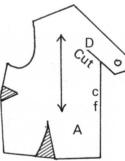

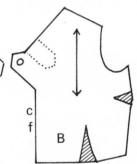

A This style must be cut with a seam up centre front, using the block with underarm dart.

1 Lay front bodice blocks together joining up centre front. 2 Draw in tabs interlocking. 3 Trace through section A on to fresh paper, cut out, and then cut along lower edge of tab to D. 4 Trace round section B as indicated on to fresh paper and cut out. The tabs must be faced before joining A and B up centre front seam.

28

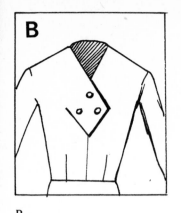

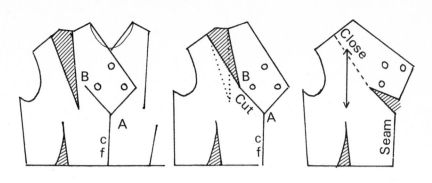

B

B

1 Place front bodice blocks together joining up centre front. 2 Draw round, and draw in cross-over front fastening. Mark lower edge of cross-over A and B. 3 Alter direction of bust dart, so that its point touches B. 4 Cut out, then cut from A along to B. 5 Close bust dart transferring dart fullness to line AB. Cut each side of the bodice in this manner. There is now plenty of space for seam allowance when cutting out; when the tab is stitched to the centre front bodice piece it should fit the bust line as the shoulder dart fitting is now transferred to the lower edge of the tab.

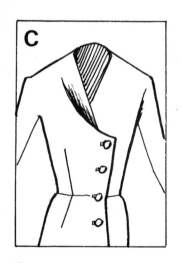

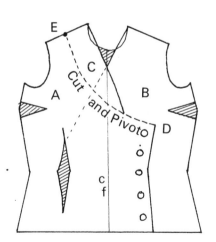

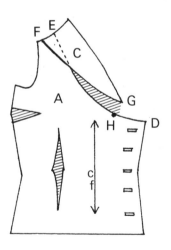

C

C

1 Lay bodice blocks together joining up centre front. 2 Draw in style lines extending wrap-over front to waist dart. 3 Mark in buttons and buttonholes. 4 Draw curve line of fold from D right through to E on shoulder line. 5 Extend section B to join waist dart. 6 Cut out section A and slash along line D to E detaching section C. 7 Replace C overlapping 1½ in. at E as illustrated. This causes C to spring out forming a pleat. When point G is joined to H a bold drape will form as illustrated.

One-piece sleeve draft

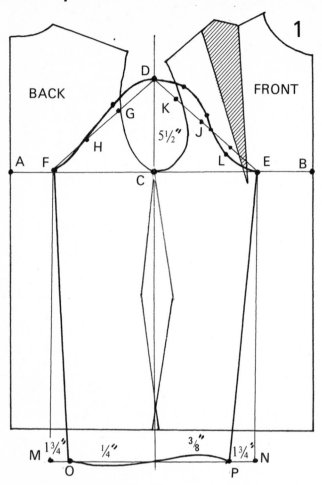

BACK   **FRONT**   **1**

Diagram 1 The sleeve draft is based on the armhole measurement.

1 Place back and front blocks together, with bust line lying along line AB. The 2 armholes should just touch at point C.

2 Rule a vertical line through the centre passing through C. Mark point D $5\frac{1}{2}$ in. up on this line. This is the crown height, and is estimated as being $\frac{1}{3}$ of the total armhole measure.

3 D to E equals the front armhole measure plus $\frac{1}{2}$ in. For ease = 9 in. To locate E, measure 9 in. from D, and where this measurement crosses line AB will be point E.

4 Locate F in the same way, taking the back armhole measure plus $\frac{1}{2}$ in. ease = $8\frac{1}{2}$ in.

5 To obtain crown line, rule a line from D to E and D to F. Divide line DF into 3 equal parts at H and G. Divide line DE into half at J, then subdivide each half into half again at K and L.

6 For crown curve, measure outwards $\frac{5}{8}$ in. at G and 1 in. at K. Connect these points with a curve passing through D and G and H and continuing to F, dropping $\frac{1}{4}$ in. below the line between H and F.

7 For front curve, measure outwards $\frac{3}{8}$ in. at J and $\frac{1}{2}$ in. inwards at L. Connect these points with a curved line continuing on to E. This now completes the crown line.

8 For underarm seams, square down 18 in. from E to N and F to M, then rule a line connecting M and N. Measure in $1\frac{3}{4}$ in. from M to O and again from N to P. Rule a line from F to O and E to P forming underarm seams.

9 Complete the bottom by curving $\frac{3}{8}$ in. above the line in the front, and dropping $\frac{1}{4}$ in. below the line at the back.

2

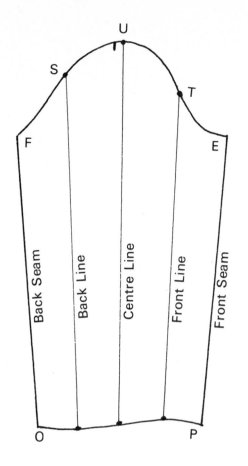

Diagram 2

1. The sleeve should now be cut out, and folded in half lengthwise. Crease firmly; this will be the centre line. Mark the crease line U.
2. Then fold the underarm seams in to meet on the centre line and crease well. Open out and mark the back crease line S and the front crease line T.
3. Make notches at S and T and draw in the back line from S and the front line from T and name these. These balance marks are used when setting a sleeve into the armhole; also the front, back and centre lines are used a great deal in cutting various types of sleeves, so these should always be marked on your sleeve block. A wrist dart may be inserted on the back line if desired.

The actual crown line measures $1\frac{1}{2}$ in. more than the armhole; this is for ease, which is distributed between S and T. Corresponding notches need to be placed on the armhole to ensure correct fitting of the sleeve.

Diagram 3

Straight sleeve block Fold sleeve in half lengthwise, bring F to E and W to V. It is most important that the underarm seams are exactly the same length; there should be no forcing the pattern to make them fit. If this is necessary, the back and front seam lines are mismatched; and this could cause the sleeve to twist. The checking of these points at this stage is essential, as this block will be the *master block* from which all your sleeves will be cut. Mark elbow halfway between V and E. Trace through elbow line on folded pattern, then open out and mark it X. A 2 in. wide wrist dart can be added up the back line, make this about 8 in. in length.

3

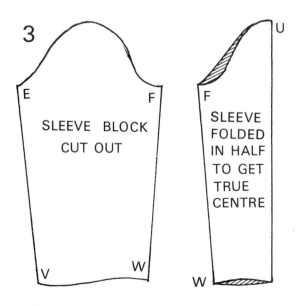

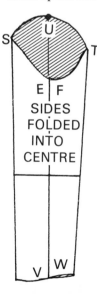

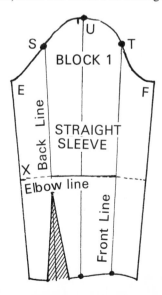

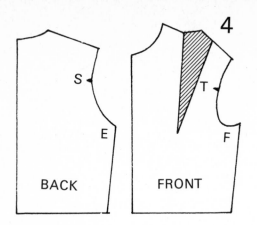

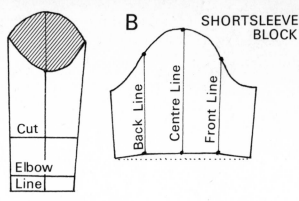

The short sleeve block

4 To locate the correct position for balance marks on front and back armholes for sleeve fitting measure the distance from F to T on front crown line, and then measure this amount on to the front armhole commencing from F. Mark this point T and notch for balance mark. To locate S repeat the process on the back armhole measuring E to S from point E.

When fitting the sleeve into the armhole, the corresponding notches must match. The excess fullness in the crown will be gathered in as ease between S and T.

Short and ¾ sleeves should never be obtained simply by cutting straight across the pattern; if you do this, the sleeve will appear too short at the back. Instead:
1 Fold the 2 underarm seams in towards the middle, the seams joining along the centre line. Crease firmly, then measure the required length down centre line from armhole and rule a line across. 2 Cut across this line, then open out the sleeve and you will find that the 2 bottom points of the underarm seams will have dropped about 1 in. forming a curved line to the base of the sleeve.

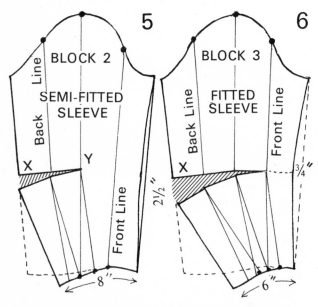

Puff sleeves

The principle of slashing and spreading is used to obtain fullness in puff sleeves.
1 Using the short sleeve block, draw round it putting in extra lines between the centre, front, and back lines. Cut up these lines from base to crown, and spread open the required fullness. Lengthen as shown about 2 in. for puffing.

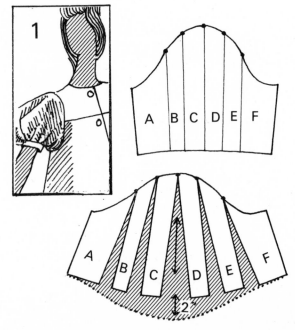

5 *Semi-fitted sleeve block* To make the semi-fitted sleeve block, cut from X through to the centre line. Fold in wrist dart, then cut up centre line from wrist to Y and overlap 1 in. at base. This will give a dart of 1½ in. at the elbow.

6 *Fitted sleeve block* At X cut through to the front sleeve line. Then cut up from the wrist on each line and overlap each line 1¼ in. until you have a dart 2½ in. wide at the elbow. The wrist will now be tight fitting. The ease at the elbow can be contributed in 3 small darts, or eased away between notches.

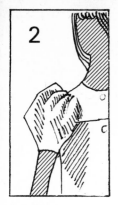

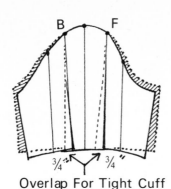

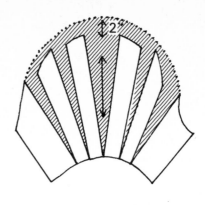

Overlap For Tight Cuff

2 In order to make the sleeve tight round the bicep, cut up front and back lines, and overlap ¾ in. at the base. Use this as your sleeve block. Draw round, add 2 extra sleeve lines parallel to front and back lines, then slash down all 5 lines from crown to base and spread open required fullness. Add about 2 in. extra height over centre of crown graduating into crown line as illustrated.

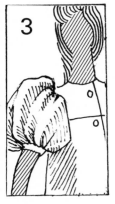

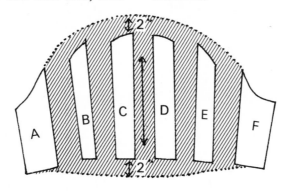

3 This is a flamboyant puff which is gathered both at the crown and at the base. Using the original short sleeve block, draw round block, and again add 2 extra sleeve lines. Cut right through all 5 lines and spread open evenly top and bottom about 2 in. as illustrated. Lay over fresh paper, and re-draw adding 2 in. extra height over centre of crown line, and 2 in. extra length in centre at base of sleeve. In making up, the sleeve will be gathered into a sleeve band at the base. The centre line of the sleeve should be placed on the straight grain of the material.

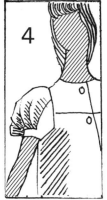

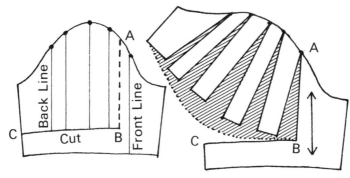

4 *Variation on the puff* This sleeve is only puffed between the front and back lines, and the cuff is cut in 1 piece with the sleeve.

· 1 Draw dotted line AB 1 in. forward from front line.
2 Mark C 2 in. up, and draw in cuff to B. 3 Cut along line AB, then slash up sleeve lines and spread open the required amount. 4 Place over fresh paper and re-draw for final pattern. Add about 2 in. extra length on to the centre and back lines for puffing.

33

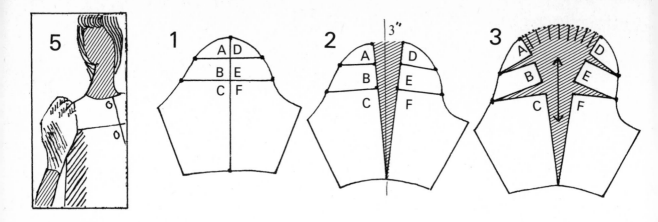

5 *Close fitting sleeve with gathered head* Here the crown is enlarged considerably, whilst the sleeve still retains a close fit round the bicep.

1 Measure down centre line 2 in. from top of crown, and rule a horizontal line across the sleeve head. Measure down another 2 in. and rule a second line across parallel to the first. 2 Letter sections A, B, C, D, E, F. 3 Slash down centre line to sleeve hem and open crown about 3 in. 4 Slash along division lines between sections from centre outwards, and push up each section about 1 in. as illustrated. This will enlarge both the height and the breadth of the crown giving about 8 in. extra for pleating. 5 Place over fresh paper and re-draw for final pattern.

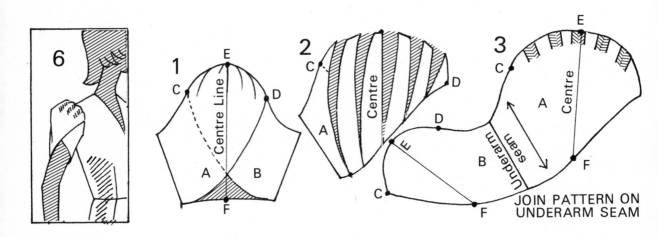

6 *Cross-over puff sleeve* This sleeve has no underarm seam. The sleeve head is extended for gathers and overlaps, forming a graceful arm opening.

1 Draw round sleeve block which has been adapted for a close fit. 2 Draw in sections A and B overlapping to points C and D. 3 Draw in gathers between C and D. 4 Trace off section ADC and cut out. Slash along fold lines from crown to hem and open each about 1 in. 5 Place over fresh paper and re-draw. Mark in centre line EF. 6 Cut out section BCED without any gathers, and lay this against section A joining sleeve along the underarm seam. Draw round this section forming 1 sleeve. Mark in centre line EF. The final pattern is now in 1 piece. When making up, first gather the sleeve head between C and D on section A, then fold sleeve under along the underarm seam so that points C, E and D are touching. The sleeve is now ready to be stitched into the armhole.

Set-in sleeves

1 *Three-quarter straight sleeve* This sleeve is widened slightly to give a straight hang. When widening do not add on to the underarm seams as this would bring the fullness against the body which is undesirable; instead, the sleeve should be slashed from the wrist up the back and front lines and opened the required amount. For a very full sleeve, slash and open the centre line as well.

1 Use the straight sleeve block and draw round making hem of sleeve about 3 in. below elbow. 2 Cut out whole sleeve, then before cutting sleeve length, fold the sleeve inwards on back and front lines so that they meet on the centre line, then cut sleeve to required length. 3 Slash up back and front lines and open 1¾ in. on each line.

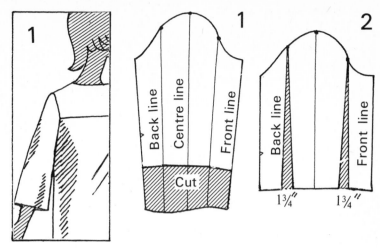

2 *Bell sleeve* This sleeve is wider, so it is cut and spread on all 3 sleeve lines, with greater fullness added to the back line. Keep the centre slash on the true straight grain. It should measure about 18 in. wide at the wrist. This sleeve may be banded at the cuff.

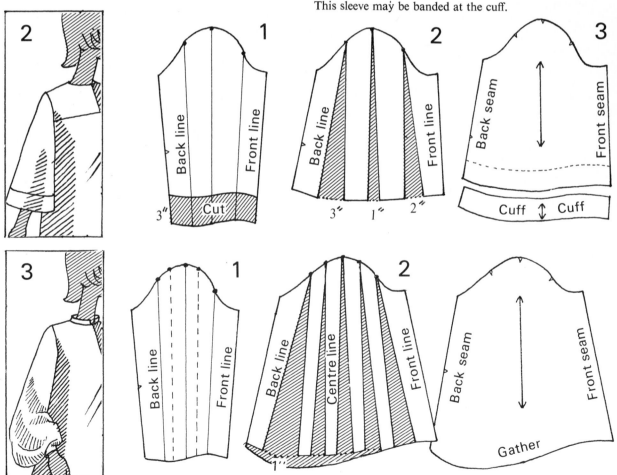

3 *Bishop sleeve* Extra length has to be added to the back of the sleeve as well as greater fullness, and it is also slashed up additional lines to spread the fullness evenly. Lower sleeve 1 in. on back line, and sparse ½ in. on front line. Re-draw on fresh paper for final sleeve.

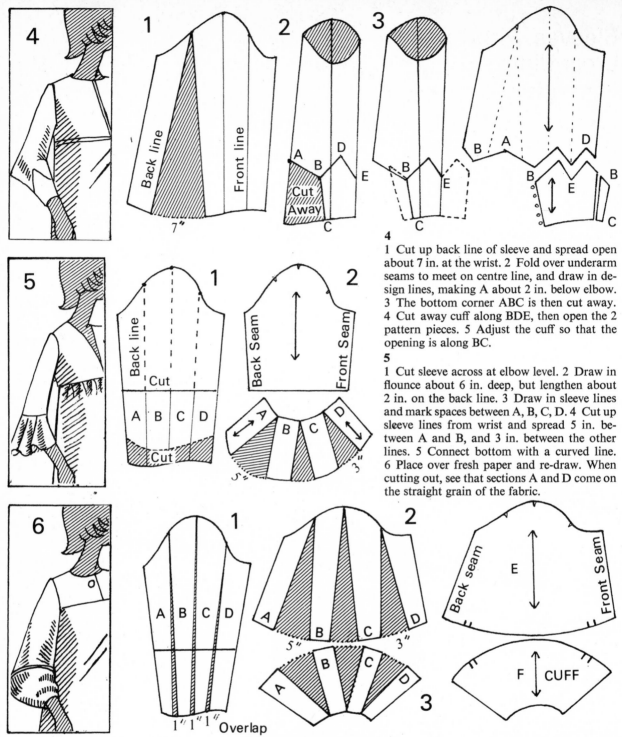

4

1 Cut up back line of sleeve and spread open about 7 in. at the wrist. 2 Fold over underarm seams to meet on centre line, and draw in design lines, making A about 2 in. below elbow. 3 The bottom corner ABC is then cut away. 4 Cut away cuff along BDE, then open the 2 pattern pieces. 5 Adjust the cuff so that the opening is along BC.

5

1 Cut sleeve across at elbow level. 2 Draw in flounce about 6 in. deep, but lengthen about 2 in. on the back line. 3 Draw in sleeve lines and mark spaces between A, B, C, D. 4 Cut up sleeve lines from wrist and spread 5 in. between A and B, and 3 in. between the other lines. 5 Connect bottom with a curved line. 6 Place over fresh paper and re-draw. When cutting out, see that sections A and D come on the straight grain of the fabric.

6 *Lantern sleeve*

1 Make a tight fitting wrist by overlapping sleeve lines 1 in. at the wrist. 2 Draw a line across 1 in. below elbow to form top of cuff. 3 Cut away cuff section, then cut up sleeve on sleeve line and spread open 5 in. between A and B, and 3 in. between other lines. 4 Repeat same process on the cuff. 5 Check that the top line of the cuff is the same measure as the bottom line of the sleeve. 6 Re-draw on fresh paper for final pattern.

Sleeves with raised crown line

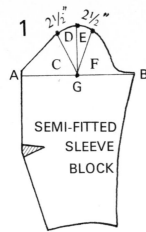

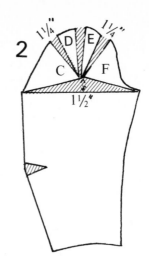

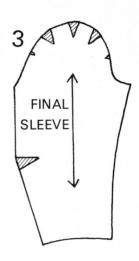

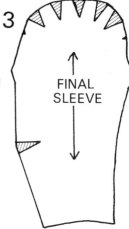

SEMI-FITTED SLEEVE BLOCK

FINAL SLEEVE

7 This has 3 darts in the head. The crown of the sleeve must be made higher and wider without the sleeve itself becoming larger.
1 Draw a line across base of armhole from A to B. Rule centre line to meet this at G. 2 Mark the 3 darts $2\frac{1}{2}$ in. apart equally each side of centre line and draw lines to G. 3 Cut down the lines to G and then along to A and B and push up $1\frac{1}{2}$ in. This raises the crown height, then open lines DEF and space out evenly 1 in. apart. 4 Mark in darts and re-draw for final sleeve.

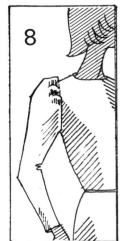

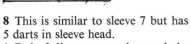

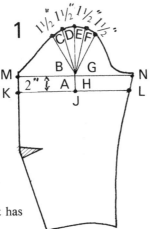

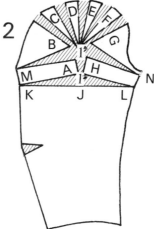

FINAL SLEEVE

8 This is similar to sleeve 7 but has 5 darts in sleeve head.
1 Rule 2 lines across the armhole, making one 2 in. below the other. 2 Mark point J where centre line crosses lower line. 3 Divide head of sleeve into 5 sections $1\frac{1}{2}$ in. apart. 4 Slash down centre line to J, then cut across to K and L and push up 1 in. 5 Slash down dart lines, then along to M and N and push up another inch. Spread open darts each 1 in. apart. 6 Place over fresh paper and re-draw for final sleeve.

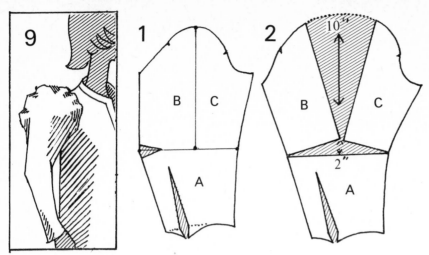

Leg-o-mutton sleeve

9 *Leg-o-mutton sleeve* This is tight fitting below the elbow, but voluminous above.

1 Cut down centre line to elbow level, then across elbow line to sleeve seams. 2 Push up 2 in. spreading the sleeve crown open about 10 in. When made up this is divided into small pleats. 3 The wrist opening is brought into the dart on the back line, and cuff extended 1 in. below the wrist as illustrated.

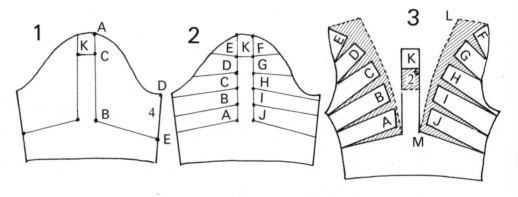

Strap sleeve

10 *Strap sleeve*

1 Draw round sleeve block. 2 Draw in strap, making it 1½ in. wide and 8 in. long between A and B. 3 Point C is 2 in. from A, square out at C and call this section K. 4 Mark point E 4 in. down from D. Connect to B. Repeat the same on other half of sleeve. 5 Divide the space between C and B into 4 equal parts, then draw division lines outwards as illustrated. 6 Cut down strap line AB, then along division lines to extremity of sleeve, and open about 1 in. between each section. In order to give the crown sufficient height, raise section K 2 in. making strap height 10 in. from A to B. 7 To give sufficient fullness to gather, 2 in. should be added at right angles to F and E. Connect L to M with a dotted line. Cut out along this line, which will be the pleating line.

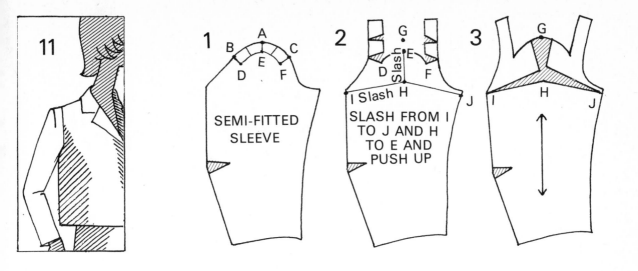

11

1 Mark A to B and A to C each 4 in. 2 Measure in 1 in. from B to D, A to E and C to F. Subdivide these sections in half again and draw inner curve. 3 Cut down from A to E and along inner curve to F and D. 4 Snip in 2 places between D and E and E and F as illustrated and raise straps until vertical. 5 Mark point G 1 in. above E, then slash from E 4 in. down to H, then slash outwards from H to I and H to J. 6 Open and push up until head of crown touches point G. Place over fresh paper and re-draw.

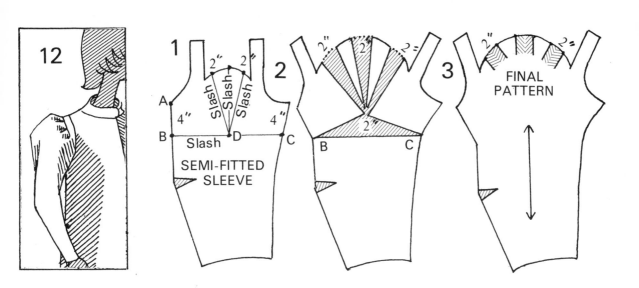

12

Extra width is added to the sleeve head to pleat into the sleeve band. Rule line BC 4 in. down from A. Slash in 3 places down to D and along to B and C. Push up 2 in. and open each vertical slash 2 in. for extra fullness as illustrated.

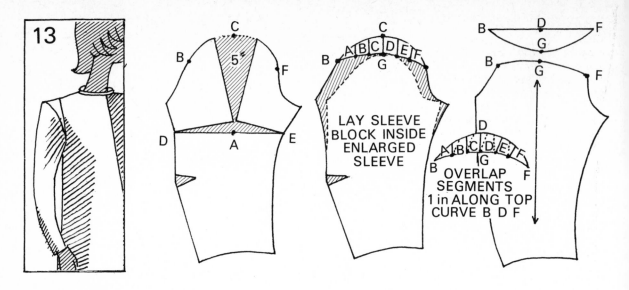

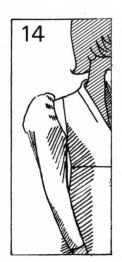

13 *Sleeve with crescent shaped head*

1 Draw round semi-fitted sleeve block and slash down from C to A, then slash across line from A to D and A to E and push up about 1 in. giving 5 in. extra fullness to sleeve head. 2 Cut out and re-draw marking point C and back and front points. 3 Place original sleeve block inside and draw round with dotted lines and mark centre top of crown G. 4 Connect BGF with a curved line, then connect BCF forming crescent. Divide crescent into 6 segments. Cut away crescent, and snip along division lines, and overlap each segment about 1 in. on outer edge of BCF. This overlapping will cause the line to become straight, which should fit the armhole between the notches. The crescent curve BGF should fit line BGF on the head of the sleeve. The crescent piece should be stiffened to give the correct stand to the head of the sleeve.

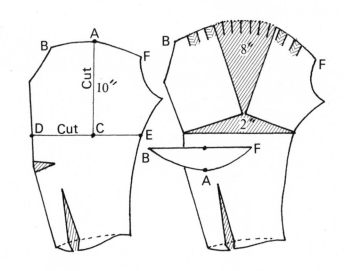

14

This is similar to sleeve 13, but has 7 small pleats inserted into the crescent head. Using the recently cut sleeve 13 as a block, cut down from A to C 10 in. then cut along from C to D, and C to E, and push up 2 in. This will give about 8 in. extra fullness between B and F which can be divided into 7 small pleats about 1 in. wide. This is then pleated in and jointed to line BAF of crescent piece.

40

15

Here the crescent is more exaggerated and extends almost to base of arm-hole. Mark points B and F about 3 in. up from underarm seams. Slash across sleeve 1 in. down from arm-hole, and 4 in. down, then slash down centre line and open up each slash 2 in. This will give about 14 in. extra fullness to the sleeve head. Draw round new sleeve and mark points BCF then mark point D 3 in. down centre line from C. Draw inner curve line of crescent from B through D to F. Divide this into 8 equal parts. Cut away crescent head, then cut along dividing lines from outer curve in-wards and overlap each segment about 2 in. Line ACF when com-pleted should equal armhole measure between notches.

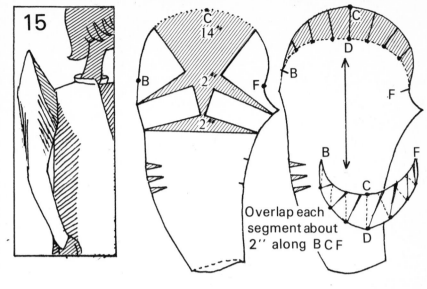

Overlap each segment about 2" along B C F

Sleeves with lowered crown line

16

Sleeves for active sport, shirt sleeves, sleeves for nurses' uniforms and tee shirts should have the depth of crown lowered from $5\frac{1}{2}$ in. to 4 in. This allows the arm to move more freely with-out the sleeve catching across the bicep muscle. This can be done without altering the actual measurement of the crown line.

1 Draw a horizontal line across the base of the crown from A to D. 2 Connect to C by curved lines from A and D. Draw lines from B and F to intersect these. 3 Cut along dotted lines from A to D up to C; then snip up to B and F and push up A and D 2 in. 4 Draw round lowered crown line, and make underarm seam parallel to original seams of sleeve block. To check crown depth, draw a line across new base of crown; it should now be 4 in. The girth of the sleeve is now 2 in. wider round the bicep, whilst still retaining the same crown line measurement.

16A

Short sleeve for active sport with crown head lowered to 4 in.

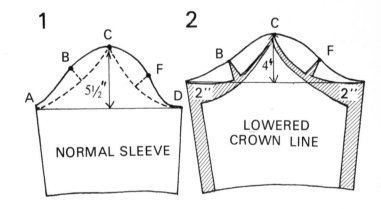

NORMAL SLEEVE

LOWERED CROWN LINE

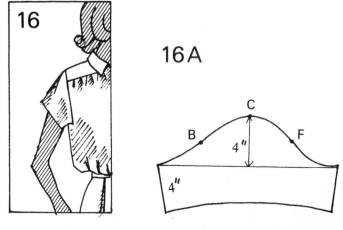

16A

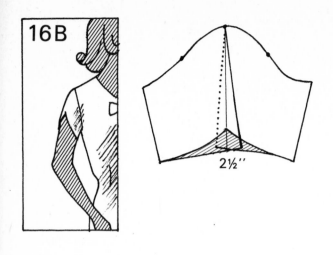

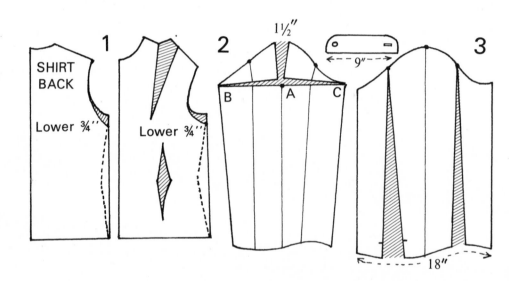

16B

Same sleeve as 16A, but the flare is taken out of the centre by cutting up centre line and overlapping 2½ in.

17 *Shirt sleeve*

Shirts have an armhole 1½ in. larger than dresses, therefore the armhole measure for a blouse, bust size 34 in., should be 18 in. The crown of the lowered headed sleeve must therefore be widened 1½ in.

1 Drop armholes ¾ in. on back and front bodice.
2 Using sleeve block with lowered crown, slash down centre line to A, then cut along to B and C and push up until sleeve head widens 1½ in. on crown line. Re-draw on fresh paper. 3 Cut up front and back lines of sleeve, and spread open until underarm seams are vertical. The wrist will then be gathered into the cuff.

Two-piece sleeve

The two-piece sleeve is mainly used for tailored clothes, suits and coats, and being shaped to the curve of the arm, gives ease of movement, combined with a close fit. This is obtained by the addition of another seam forming the sleeve into 2 parts; the under sleeve, and the upper sleeve.

1 Using the straight sleeve block, fold in the underarm seams to meet on the centre line. Mark in the elbow line. 2 Cut along elbow line from back point to within $\frac{1}{16}$ in. of the front point, and swing open 1½ in. at the elbow. 3 Place over clean paper and re-draw making the wrist measure 4 in. from H to G. Connect H to elbow with a straight line. 4 Draw round folded armhole, then measure in 1 in. from F to J and B to I. At the

elbow measure in $\frac{3}{4}$ in. and $\frac{1}{2}$ in. at the wrist. Join these points with dotted lines forming the under sleeve, diagram 3. Trace on to fresh paper for final sleeve, diagram 4. 5 To complete upper sleeve, take the original folded sleeve and lay the top half over sleeve draft 3 with point C touching. Mark in points J and I. With tracing wheel, trace down from I and J to elbow line; then open out along folded lines and cut up the newly traced lines. Add $\frac{1}{2}$ in. on to each side of the wrist and join to elbow.

This is now the upper sleeve, diagram 5. Diagram 6 shows the relationship between the upper and the under sleeves. The back seam of the upper sleeve is 1 in. longer than the back seam of the under sleeve, this amount being eased away between the balance marks at the elbow. The wrist of the under sleeve will now measure 3 in. and the upper sleeve 5 in. If a narrower wrist measure is required, the sleeve can be taken in on the seams.

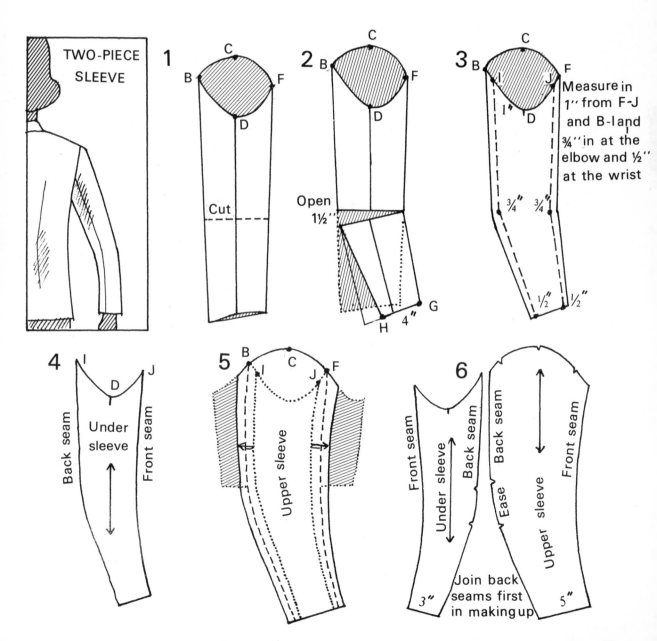

How to adjust the blocks for shoulder pads

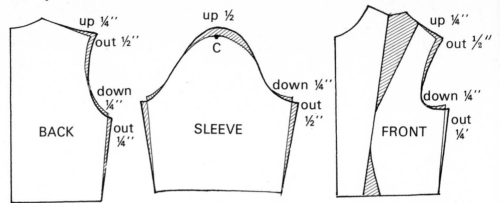

up ¼''
out ½''
down ¼''
out ¼''

BACK

up ½
C
down ¼''
out ½''

SLEEVE

up ¼''
out ½''
down ¼''
out ¼'

FRONT

Drop shoulders

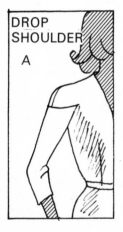

DROP SHOULDER A

Drop shoulder A These three styles look decidedly better if the shoulder is slightly padded, therefore adapt your bodice and sleeve blocks as shown in the diagram above before cutting the pattern.

Raise back and front blocks ¼ in. on shoulder tips, and widen ½ in. Lower armhole and widen armhole ¼ in. Draw in new armhole and taper side seam to nothing at the waist. Adjust sleeve by raising crown ½ in. at C and lowering it ¼ in. at the armhole. It should also be widened here ½ in. Draw in new crown line. Draw in new underarm seam graduating into sleeve seam as shown.

1 Make the *cap* of the sleeve 3½ in. deep. It should never be deeper than this, but it can be shorter if desired. Measure 3½ in. from shoulder point down front and back armhole. Mark these points J and K. 2 Measure this amount on crown each side of C and mark these points B and F. Mark point D 3½ in. down from C. 3 Connect BDE with a curved line. Rule in centre line and mark back cap G and front cap H. 4 Cut away G and H from sleeve and place against bodice armholes with points B and F joining J and K with C ¼–½ in. cap from shoulder point. Re-draw round bodice and sleeve cap together for final pattern.

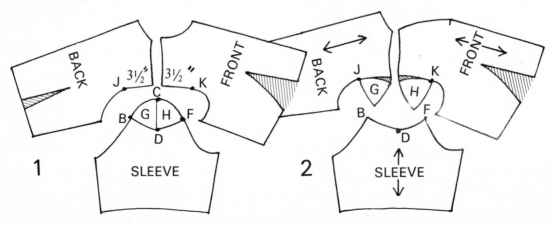

BACK J 3½'' 3½'' K FRONT
B G H F
C
D
1 SLEEVE

BACK J K FRONT
B G H F
D
2 SLEEVE

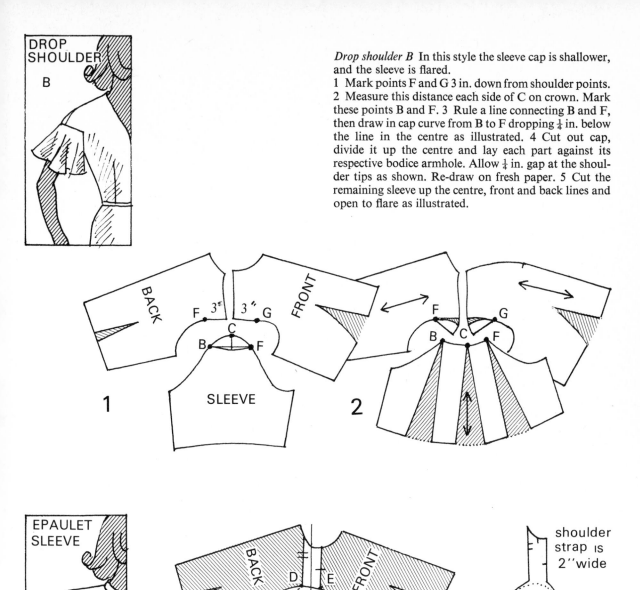

DROP
SHOULDER

B

Drop shoulder B In this style the sleeve cap is shallower, and the sleeve is flared.
1 Mark points F and G 3 in. down from shoulder points.
2 Measure this distance each side of C on crown. Mark these points B and F. 3 Rule a line connecting B and F, then draw in cap curve from B to F dropping $\frac{1}{4}$ in. below the line in the centre as illustrated. 4 Cut out cap, divide it up the centre and lay each part against its respective bodice armhole. Allow $\frac{1}{4}$ in. gap at the shoulder tips as shown. Re-draw on fresh paper. 5 Cut the remaining sleeve up the centre, front and back lines and open to flare as illustrated.

BACK
FRONT
F   3"   3"   G
B   C   F
SLEEVE
1

F   G
B   C   F
2

EPAULET
SLEEVE

BACK
FRONT
D   E
B   C
F
SLEEVE

Place blocks
shoulder points
meeting ¼
above point c

shoulder
strap is
2" wide

B   F
SLEEVE

Epaulet sleeve
1 Draw round sleeve block and extend centre line 6 in. above point C. 2 Lay front and back bodice blocks with shoulder seams touching along extended centre line $\frac{1}{2}$ in. up from point C. 3 Draw epaulet strap making it 2 in. wide. 4 Extend head of sleeve to join strap point D and E. Place balance marks on strap lines for correct fitting.
5 Place over clean sheet of paper and trace round the outline of the sleeve and strap combined. 6 Cut out for final pattern.

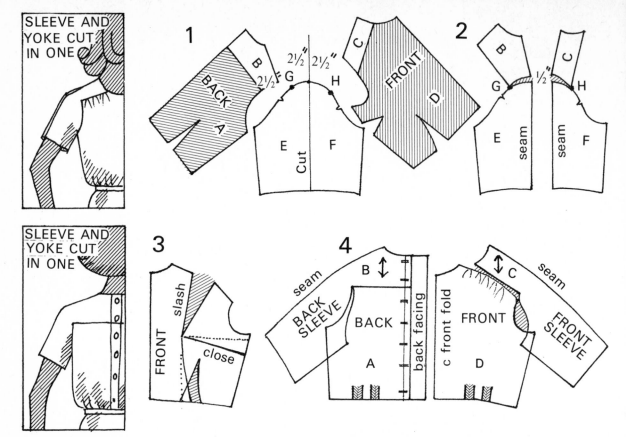

Sleeve and yoke cut in one

1 Draw round front and back bodice blocks marking in shoulder yoke. Do not make this deeper than 2½ in. Mark bodice sections A and D and yoke sections B and C. 2 Draw round sleeve block, putting in centre line. 3 Mark points G and H, 2½ in. each side of C. 4 Cut the sleeve in half down centre line. Cut away yokes from bodice and place over head of sleeve allowing ½ in.–1 in.

gap between C and yoke shoulder point, and bottom corner of yoke touching G and H. 5 Trace round sleeve and yoke in 1 piece. 6 Transfer underarm dart fullness to front bodice yoke line as shown in diagram 3. Diagram 4 shows the relationship of sections B and C to the bodice front and back. The yokes must be placed on the straight grain of the fabric, the sleeve then being cut on the bias grain.

Raglan sleeves

A *The classic raglan sleeve*
1 Rule straight lines from A to D and H to E making A and H 1 in. from neck point. Points D and E should be about ⅔ way down armhole. 2 Draw a gently curved line over both AD and HE rising ½ in. over AD and ¼ in. over HE as illustrated. 3 Put in balance marks across curve. 4 Cut away raglan sections. 5 Draw round sleeve block extending the centre line 7 in. above C. Mark point G ½ in. up from C and place 2 dots ¼ in. each side of G. 6 Lay the raglan sections over crown line with shoulder tips touching these dots, and points D and E resting on sleeve crown line as illustrated. 7 Continue shoulder lines to point C forming a large dart. This can be lengthened ½ in. if so desired. As there is now no seam over the crown of the sleeve in which to distribute the ease, it will be seen that about 1 in. of ease is taken out by the shoulder dart. The rest of the ease should be distributed along the front and back raglan seam lines, which can be shrunk away and ensures a good fit.

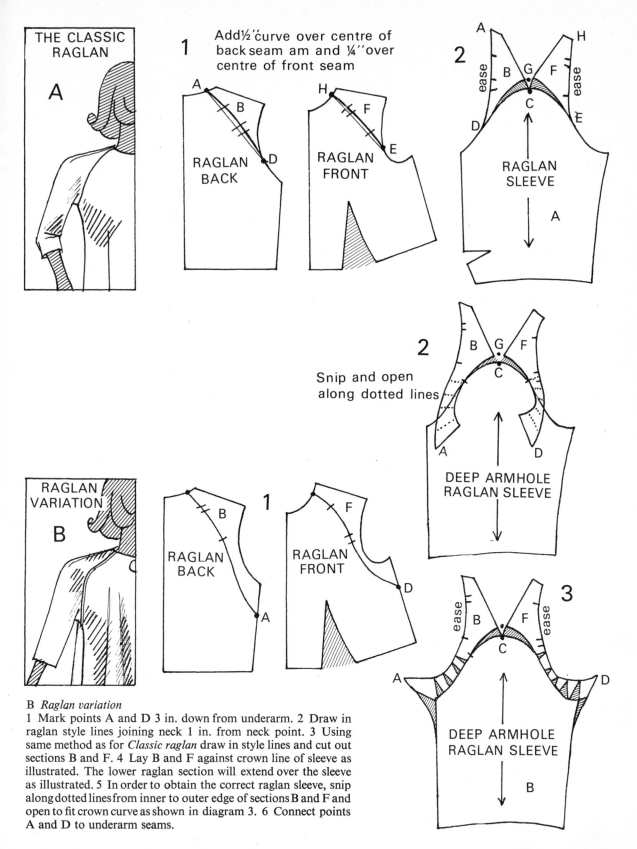

THE CLASSIC RAGLAN

A

1 Add ½" curve over centre of back seam am and ¼" over centre of front seam

A B D
RAGLAN BACK

H F E
RAGLAN FRONT

2
A B G F H
ease ease
C
D E
RAGLAN SLEEVE
A

2
Snip and open along dotted lines
B G F
C
A D
DEEP ARMHOLE RAGLAN SLEEVE

RAGLAN VARIATION

B

1
B
RAGLAN BACK
A

F
RAGLAN FRONT
D

3
A B F D
ease ease
C
DEEP ARMHOLE RAGLAN SLEEVE
B

B *Raglan variation*

1 Mark points A and D 3 in. down from underarm. 2 Draw in raglan style lines joining neck 1 in. from neck point. 3 Using same method as for *Classic raglan* draw in style lines and cut out sections B and F. 4 Lay B and F against crown line of sleeve as illustrated. The lower raglan section will extend over the sleeve as illustrated. 5 In order to obtain the correct raglan sleeve, snip along dotted lines from inner to outer edge of sections B and F and open to fit crown curve as shown in diagram 3. 6 Connect points A and D to underarm seams.

Deep armhole raglan: alternative method

C Raglan

1 Extend back shoulder length $\frac{1}{2}$ in., lower armhole $2\frac{1}{2}$ in. Connect to shoulder with dotted line. 2 Raise and extend front shoulder $\frac{1}{2}$ in. Drop armhole $2\frac{1}{2}$ in. Draw in new armhole. 3 Point D is $\frac{1}{2}$ in. above C. Place raglan sections on top of crown line. 3B Mark points H 4 in. from J and G 4 in. from I. Cut up from J to H and I to G, then snip to sleeve seams and open $2\frac{1}{2}$ in. 4 Final sleeve showing $2\frac{1}{2}$ in. extra length on underarm seam. The extra length should always correspond to the amount lowered at armhole.

RAGLAN C

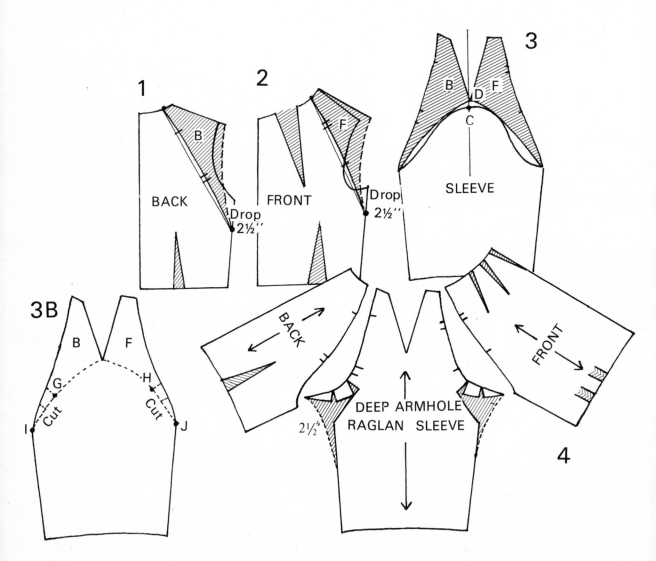

48

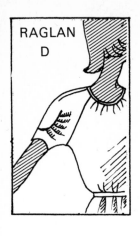

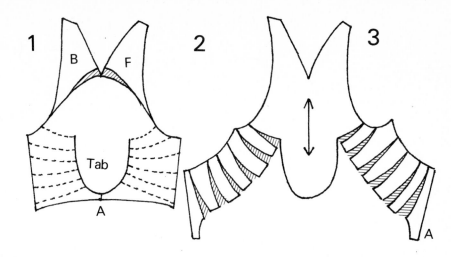

D *Raglan*

1 Draft *Classic raglan sleeve*. 2 Draw in tab feature, and lines of folds. 3 From point A cut up to and round tab. Then cut along dotted lines from tab to underarm seams and open required amount for folds. 4 Place over fresh paper and re-draw for final pattern.

E *Raglan bishop sleeve*

1 Draw round *Classic raglan* sleeve block, and mark in centre, back, and front lines. 2 Cut up centre, back and front lines from wrist to armhole and spread out required amount at wrist. When this is gathered into the wristband it will appear as shown in diagram E.

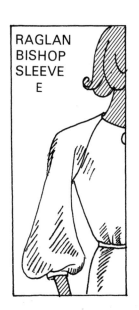

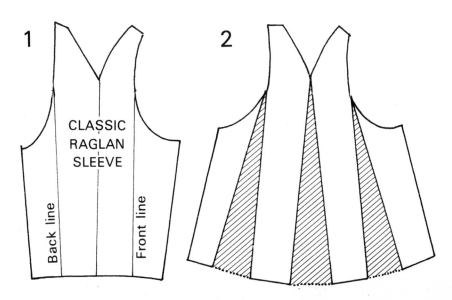

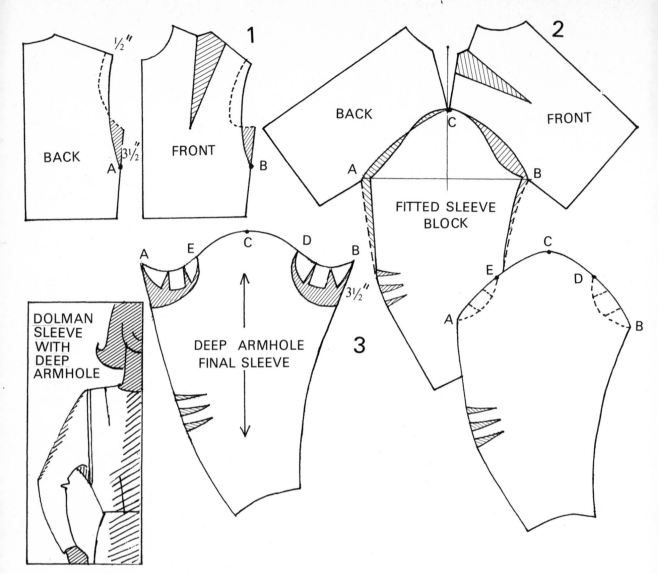

Batwing and Dolman sleeves

Dolman sleeve with deep armhole

All batwing and dolman sleeves have a deep armhole. It is therefore necessary to lower the arm on the bodice blocks prior to cutting the pattern.

1 Widen shoulders $\frac{1}{2}$ in. Deepen armholes $3\frac{1}{2}$ in. Connect A and B to shoulder with a curved line and cut out. 2 Lay back and front bodice over sleeve block with shoulder points touching at C, and equally balanced on each side as illustrated. Connect A and B to sleeve seam with a dotted line. Cut out new sleeve. 3 In order to give sufficient room for movement, the underarm seam must now be lengthened $3\frac{1}{2}$ in. Mark points D and E halfway between CB and CA. Then draw a semicircular curve from B to D and A to E. Slash along curve making snips to spread, and push up $3\frac{1}{2}$ in. as shown in diagram 3. Re-draw on fresh paper for final sleeve.

Square armhole

1 Drop armhole $2\frac{1}{2}$ in. Draw in new square armhole.
2 Lengthen jacket 2 in. at hem, and straighten side
seams for unfitted line. 3 Draw round sleeve block putting in centre line, and draw a horizontal line across
base of crown line. Lay back and front blocks over sleeve
with shoulder points meeting on C and points A and B
resting equidistant each side of sleeve on horizontal line.
It is important that these are symmetrical. Connect A
and B to sleeve with a curved line. Cut out sleeve
following round new square crown line. It is now necessary to add $2\frac{1}{2}$ in. extra length to the underarm seam for
ease of movement. 4 Mark points G and H midway be-
tween DE and DF. Cut a curved line from A to G and
B to H and push up $2\frac{1}{2}$ in. Connect A and B to sleeve
seam with curved lines as illustrated.

SQUARE
ARMHOLE

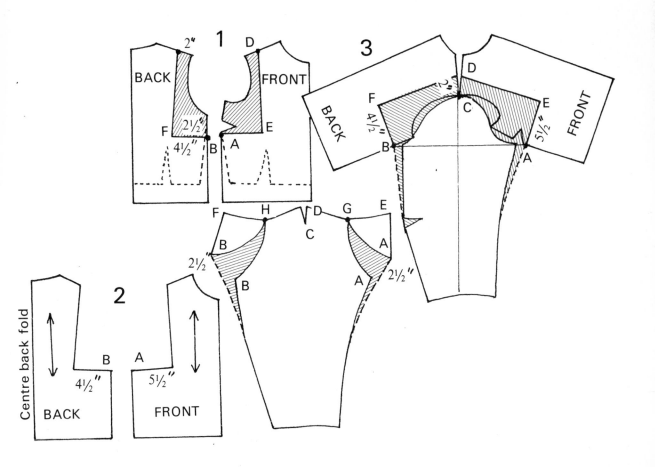

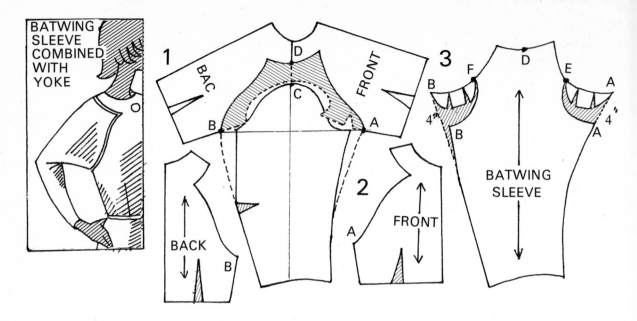

Batwing sleeve combined with yoke

1 Draw style lines of armhole on bodice front and back, making A and B $4\frac{1}{2}$ in. up from waist line, and point D 2 in. from shoulder point. Lay bodices over top of sleeve crown line with shoulder points touching at C and A and B equidistant each side of the sleeve, resting on the horizontal line. Connect A and B to sleeve seams with a curved line. 2 Cut out sleeve, following round the new lines of the sleeve head. 3 4 in. extra length must now be added to underarm sleeve seam. Mark points E and F halfway between D and A and D and B. Cut a curve from A to E and B to F, snip to the outer seam in 2 places, and push up 4 in. Connect the newly raised points A and B to the sleeve seam with a curved line. This gives extra width as well as extra length to the sleeve.

Square armhole: Alternative method
1 Lengthen bodices 2 in. below waist, and straighten side seams. Move shoulder dart to the neck making A $2\frac{1}{2}$ in. from neck point. Raise front shoulder $\frac{1}{2}$ in. at the shoulder point. 2 Draw in yoke, making points G and E 3 in. below armhole. Mark point D $5\frac{1}{2}$ in. from E, and H 5 in. from G. Join H to F which is $1\frac{1}{2}$ in. from centre back. 3 Draw round sleeve block raising centre line 8 in. beyond C and rule a cross line through base of armhole. Place bodices over sleeve with shoulder points touching C and points E and G resting on the cross line. Mark points I and J midway between DE and GH. 4 In order to give ease of movement, a simulated gusset is obtained by squaring down from J and I the exact measurement of the remaining yoke line. 5 Mark these points K and L and connect to underarm seam with a curved line. 6 The final sleeve is obtained by tracing round sleeve combined with bodice yokes.

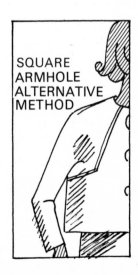

SQUARE ARMHOLE ALTERNATIVE METHOD

Square armhole: Alternative method

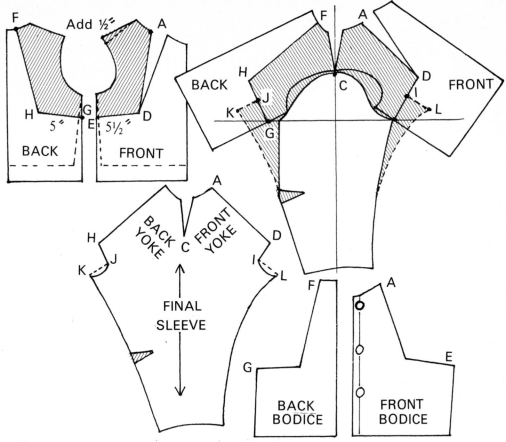

Dolman sleeve with curved front yoke and deep armhole at the back

1 Drop back armhole 3 in. to point A. Join A to shoulder point with gently curved line. Draw yoke on bodice front, curving from neck point to D 3 in. below armhole. Draw in neck opening and gather on bodice front. 2 Place bodices over sleeve, with points A and D resting on cross line, and shoulder points meeting at C.

Mark E 4½ in. up from A on line AB. Point F is 3 in. from A. Join F to E with a curved line. 3 Mark point H on front yoke 5 in. from D. Trace curve line D to H. Then reverse tracing so that point D rests on cross line 3 in. away. Call this point G. Connect both F and G to underarm seams with a curved line. 4 Trace off sleeve and front yoke separately. Final sleeve pattern shows front yoke joining at point C with a deep armhole at the back.

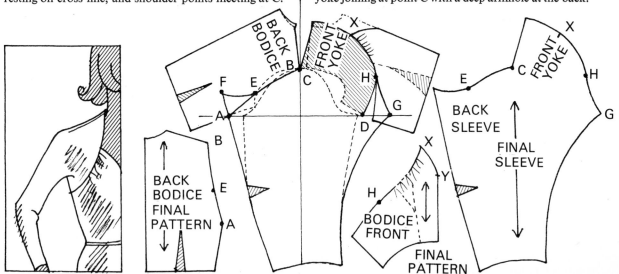

Kimono sleeves

Kimono sleeves are cut in 1 piece with the bodice, and therefore lose the original curve of the lower armhole. As the underarm seam and the bodice side seam join and become 1 seam, it is necessary to centralize the bodice side seam. Lay bodice front and back together joining along the side seam, as in diagram 1. Measure across the girth of the 2 bodices from centre front to centre back and mark A midway between. Rule line from A to the waist parallel to the side seam. The side seam is now centralized. Raise front shoulder point $\frac{1}{2}$ in. so that armholes are equal, then cut out separate front and back bodice. The centre line of the sleeve should be moved $\frac{5}{8}$ in. towards the back at the waist. This will form the new outside sleeve seam which is best cut on the bias.

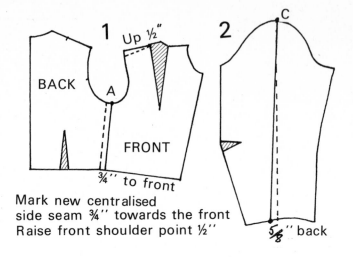

Mark new centralised
side seam ¾'' towards the front
Raise front shoulder point ½''

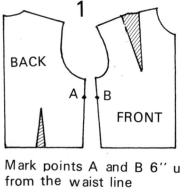

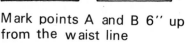

Mark points A and B 6'' up
from the waist line

1 Kimono sleeve without gusset

1 Mark points A and B on side seams 6 in. up from the waist. 2 Draw round semi-fitted sleeve block allowing 8 in. above point C. Rule line E to D across sleeve crown 2 in. up from base of crown. 3 Lay bodice blocks above sleeve head, with points A and B resting on line ED 4 in. away from crown curve, and pivot, so that the back and front shoulder points lie 1 in. above top of crown. The amount of space between shoulder seams may vary a little, as bodice blocks are individual. Raise both back and front shoulder points $\frac{1}{2}$ in. and continue lines to join sleeve centre line about $1\frac{1}{2}$ in. below C. This will form a shoulder dart. 4 Connect underarm sleeve seams to bodice back and front as illustrated, joining the bodice just below A and B. 5 Lay over fresh paper and trace off front and back separately. This will give you the kimono bodice and sleeve in one piece. The shaded areas in diagram 3 show the necessary drape to allow ease of movement.

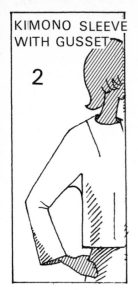

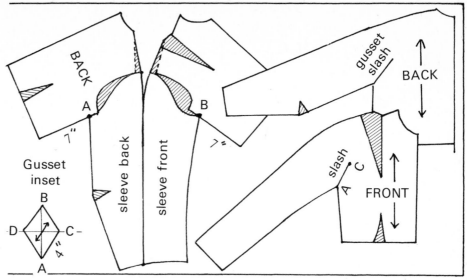

2 Kimono sleeve with gusset

It is necessary to insert a gusset under the arm to give extra length to the underarm seam, to ensure ease of movement. Whenever the angle of the junction of the side seam with the underarm seam is less than a right angle, a gusset should be inserted to enable the arm to be raised without pulling up the waist line.

1 Mark points A and B 7 in. up from the waist. 2 Lay bodice back and front against sleeve with A and B touching top of underarm seam, and shoulder points touching crown line as illustrated. 3 Add 1 in. height to shoulder points and re-draw shoulder line continuing into sleeve centre line, dividing the sleeve into 2 separate pieces—the sleeve front and the sleeve back. 4 Trace round both front and back bodice and sleeve pieces separately. 5 Back and front final patterns show gusset slash 3 in. long. How to obtain gusset slash is shown in sleeve No. 5.

3 Tight fitting kimono sleeve with gusset

For the tight fitting kimono, use the fitted sleeve block. In order to give an uncluttered line to the sleeve with no wrinkling from the underarm seam, the angle of the underarm seam to the bodice side seam must be more acute. This necessitates the insertion of a 4–5 in. gusset.

1 Mark points A and B on bodice side seam 5 in. up from the waist line. 2 Draw round fitted sleeve block, and lay bodice front and back against sleeve crown with points A and B coming 1½ in. below armhole, and shoulder points touching crown line. 3 Add 1 in. height to each shoulder point. Re-draw shoulder line, continuing on to sleeve centre line. In order to get a close fit at the wrist, reduce wrist measure on the centre line as illustrated. 4 Trace round both bodice and sleeve combined, and cut out forming separate front and back patterns. A gusset has now to be inserted under the arm.

Gusset insertion Gussets are square or diamond shaped. To obtain a diamond shaped gusset for a 4 in. slash: A Rule vertical line 6½ in. long. Mark this AB. B Rule horizontal line across centre of AB. C Lay a ruler at point A so that the measurement of 4 in. strikes the horizontal line. Mark this point C. D Repeat the same on opposite side, and mark this D. Connect D and C to B. The vertical line AB should be cut on the true bias.

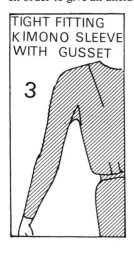

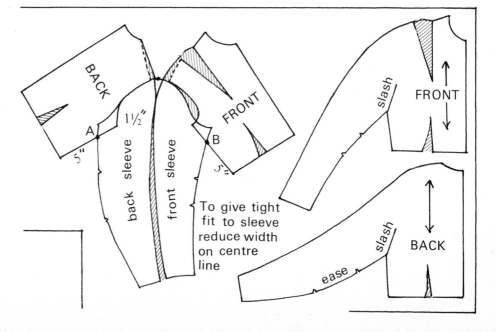

To give tight fit to sleeve reduce width on centre line

Additional notes on the construction of kimono sleeves

Diagram 4 shows an alternative method of drafting the kimono sleeve. This draft requires shoulder padding and a gusset insertion under the arm.

Diagram 5 shows how to obtain the correct direction for the gusset slash. This will vary in direction according to individual sleeve and bodice drafts, but the construction line A to B should always be ruled from the junction of the under-arm seam and the side seam, through the deepest curve of the armhole to the shoulder. A to C is length of gusset slash, which should be about 3 in.

Diagram 6 shows how the draft for the normal kimono sleeve with underarm gusset can be adapted to a sleeve with more drape from shoulder, to enable more freedom of movement, without the insertion of a gusset.

5 *How to obtain correct direction for gusset slash*
To obtain the correct angle for the gusset slash, rule a line from point A passing through the deepest curve of the armhole to the shoulder. Then measure 3 in. up from A to C. This is the slash opening. Slash from A to C to insert gusset. This should be done on both front and back patterns.

4 *Alternative method of drafting kimono sleeve*
1 Divide sleeve in half down centre line. 2 Lay sleeve back and sleeve front against bodice back and front as illustrated. 3 Connect point C to neck point forming new shoulder line.

This will give a high square shoulder requiring padding. For natural shoulders, cut along dotted line as indicated in the diagram.

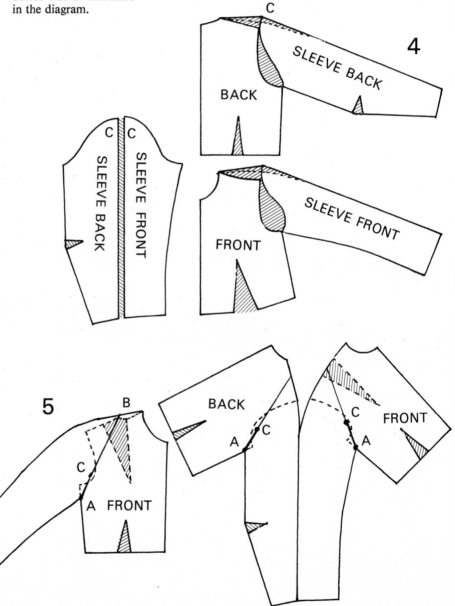

6 *Adaptation of kimono block for sleeve with no gusset*

Slash from junction of underarm seam and side seam up to shoulder point and open 2–3 in. This will allow more drape for ease of movement without a gusset inset. Do the same to both front and back patterns. Lay on fresh paper and re-draw for final patterns.

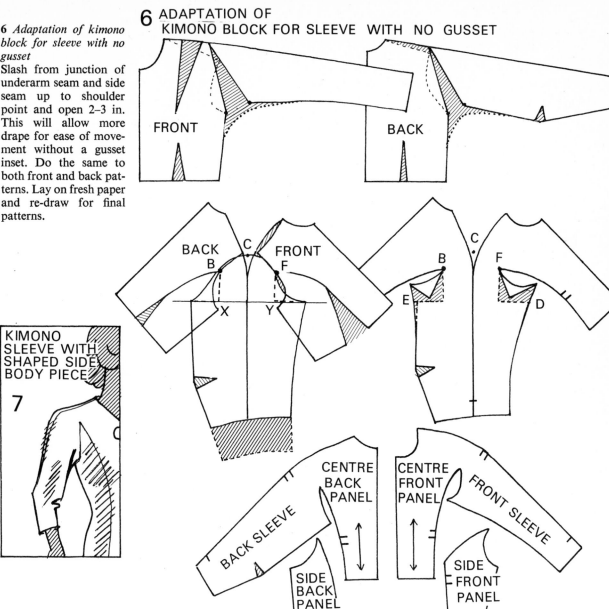

7 *Kimono sleeve with shaped side body piece*

1 Draw round sleeve block making it ¾ length. 2 Draw horizontal line through base of crown. 3 Lay bodice blocks against crown of sleeve placed so that points X and Y come 1 in. below the horizontal line, and 3½ in. in from the underarm seam as illustrated. 4 Continue the shoulder lines into the sleeve centre line, raising front shoulder ½ in. and forming a dart at point C. 5 Measuring 4 in. down from C, mark points B and F on armhole. 6 Draw side panel seam by drawing a curved line from dart points to B and F. 7 Drop a vertical line from B and F to join horizontal line forming right angle. 8 Trace off side panel pieces, disregarding the sleeve. 9 Cut out centre front and back panel with the sleeve, then cut up the centre line of the sleeve separating front from back. 10 To allow ease of movement cut along dotted lines from E up to B and D up to F and push up 2½ in. to within ⅜ in. of panel side seam. 11 Re-draw for final pattern.

8 *Sleeve with kimono back and set-in front*

1 Lower bodice armholes 1 in. front and back. 2 Draw round straight sleeve block and extend crown line 1 in. at B and F. 3 Place bodice back against sleeve crown with point B touching lowered base of armhole. 4 Raise back shoulder point 1 in. and continue shoulder line into sleeve centre line. 5 Mark points D and F and connect with dotted line forming right angle. 6 In order to lengthen the underarm seam, slash from B up to shoulder point on kimono back and open 3 in. then slash from F up to D and open 3 in. 7 Re-draw on fresh paper for final pattern, which comprises the back and sleeve cut in 1 piece, and the front bodice as a separate piece. When cutting out, place centre back on the straight grain of the fabric.

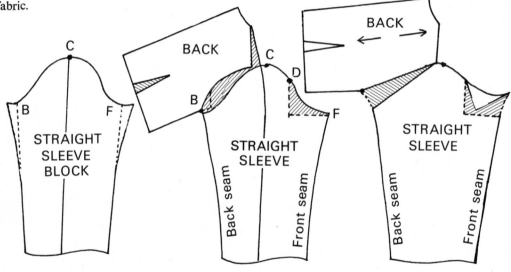

Tailored skirt draft

Waist 26 in.
Hips 37 in.
Length 25 in.

The tailored skirt is constructed to fit the waist tightly, and has only 1 in. ease allowance on the hip line. It should hang pencil slim, with the side seam which is placed midway between the centre front and back hanging perpendicular from waist to hem. 1½ in. spring is allowed on the side seam at G for striding room. If more striding room is required it can be added to the centre front and back of the skirt by the insertion of pleats, panel seams, godets and flares, etc, examples of which are illustrated in the following section. The skirt draft as it stands is perfectly suitable for a short slim skirt allowing enough room for movement without the addition of pleats. In the tailored skirt, the side seam is always centralized and should only be used for cutting skirts for tailored suits and costumes or to combine with the kimono bodice where the side seam has already been centralized. It is essential to use the tailored skirt blocks when adapting the skirt block for culottes and trouser block. This is explained fully in the section on casual wear.

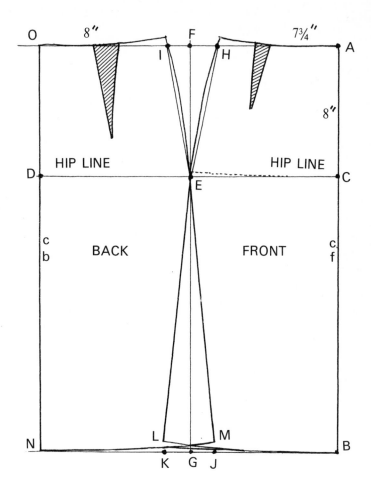

Draft for front and back skirt block

1 Rule line AB making it 25 in. long.
2 Mark point C 8 in. from A.
3 Square out at A, B and C.
4 C to D is half hip measurement + ½ in. ease = 19 in.
5 Point E is midway between CD.
6 Rule vertical line through E crossing line A at F and line B at G.
7 Square up and down at D forming centre back line.
8 For front waist line, measure from A to H ¼ waist measure + 1 in. for dart, and ¼ in. for ease = 7¾ in.
9 Place dart 2½ in. in from side seam, making it 1 in. wide and 4 in. long. Slope dart parallel to side seam.
10 At H raise ¼ in. and draw in waist curve.
11 Rule construction line from H to E, then draw a gently curved line for the hip.
12 Add 1½ in. spring on hem line at G. Mark this K then mark L ¼ in. up from K.
13 Draw in hem line from L gently curving down to B.
14 Raise hip line ¼ in. above point E and gently curve towards C.
15 Locate point I by measuring ¼ waist measure + 1½ in. from O = 8 in.
16 Connect I to E adding slight curve for hip.
17 Mark point J 1½ in. from G.
18 Mark point M ¼ in. up from J.
19 Connect E to M forming side seam, then draw in hem line.
20 Measure up ¼ in. at I and draw in waist line curve.
21 Place back dart 3 in. from side seam, making it 1½ in. wide, and 6 in. long.
22 Raise hip line ¼ in. at point E and draw as a curved line.
23 Trace through back and front separately for final patterns.

Basic skirt block

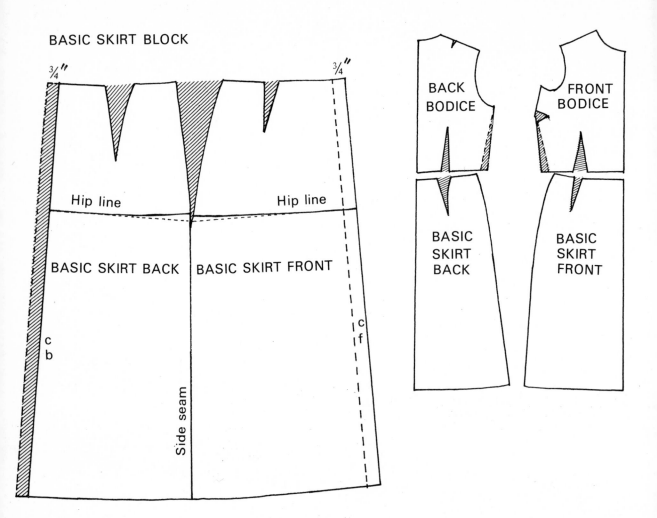

BASIC SKIRT BLOCK

¾″ ¾″

Hip line   Hip line

BASIC SKIRT BACK   BASIC SKIRT FRONT

Side seam

c
b

c
f

BACK BODICE   FRONT BODICE

BASIC SKIRT BACK   BASIC SKIRT FRONT

The tailored skirt block can quite easily be adapted to a *basic skirt block* which can be used in conjunction with the bodice block. In dresses, the front side seam is taken ¾ in. round towards the back and if you measure the waists of the bodice blocks, you will find that the front will be ¾ in. wider than the back—therefore the basic skirt block should be altered to fit the bodice. In the diagram you will notice that the completed basic skirt is in each case 1 in. smaller on the waist than the bodice—this is correct, for the separate skirt is always made to fit tightly and has only 1 in. ease round the waist. If these are joined together to form a dress block a compromise can be made by widening the skirt to fit the bodice at the waist, then shaping in the side seam on a graceful line.

How to adapt tailored skirt into basic skirt block
1 Lay front and back skirt blocks together with side seams touching. 2 Check hem line curve, and see that the hip line is parallel to the hem line. This will give a curved hip line which is correct—see dotted line in diagram. 3 Remove ¾ in. from centre back and add this amount on to centre front. 4 Cut up side seam making separate front and back patterns. In styles where there is no side seam, the skirt block can be joined up the side seam as shown. This is helpful when cutting patterns where a style line on the front continues round to the back of the skirt.

Pleated skirts

In these three skirts, the waist dart is eliminated into the hip yoke, giving style and fit.

1 *Inverted pleat* Pleat paper first for inverted pleat, then lay centre front of block against the fold. To avoid a seam in the centre of the pleat a separate inset is cut, the join then coming either side of the pleat opening, does not show.

1 Rule a line 2½ in. in from edge of paper, the full length of the skirt. 2 Fold paper under on line. 3 Place centre front of skirt block against the fold and draw round. 4 Draw in hip yoke. 5 Cut out, then cut along hip yoke separating the skirt from the yoke. 6 Pin in dart and re-draw yoke. 7 Cut pleat inset, making it 5 in. wide and same length as pleat.

2 *Box pleat* This skirt has 6 box pleats hanging from a curved hip yoke. The box pleats are very slightly flared to give striding room.

1 Draw round skirt block putting in hip yoke, and straighten side seam as illustrated. 2 Draw in centre panel, marking pleat 3¼ in. from centre front at the top, and 5 in. from centre front at the hem. Panel A, the side panel, should measure 6½ in. at the top and 10 in. at hem level. 3 Cut out, then cut away yoke and close the dart. 4 Cut up pleat lines and open same width of panels for box pleating,

e.g. 6½ in. at top and 10 in. at hem. Rule line Q up the middle of the pleat. When making the box pleat the panel lines should meet on line Q. In this style the skirt is also pleated on the side seam.

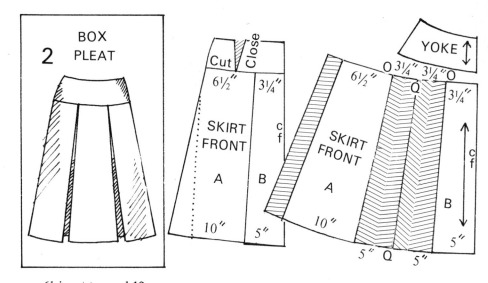

3 *Knife pleats* In this style, the centre front panel and yoke are cut in 1 piece. The knife pleats are slightly flared for striding room. The band at the top of the pleat simulates a pocket. 1 Draw round skirt block, marking in yoke and knife pleats. Make pleats 2 in. wide at the top widening to 3 in. at the hem. 2 Rule new side seam parallel to pleats. 3 Cut out, then slash along yoke from G to H then cut away pleat section. 4 Cut up pleat lines and spread open for pleats as illustrated. 5 Place over fresh paper and re-draw join-

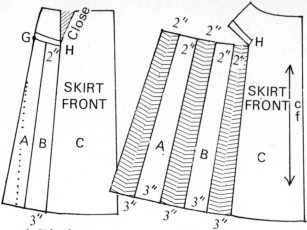

3 KNIFE PLEATS

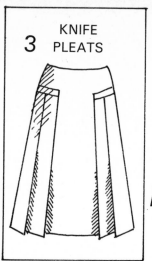

ing pleats to skirt front panel. The hem is now slightly flared with the pleats falling slightly on the bias grain which will give softness to the pleat.

4 *Side pleats*
1 Place skirt front and back together, joining along side seam. 2 Draw in panel inset with 6 pleats each 2 in. wide. Letter these A to F. 3 Cut away panel inset, and close waist darts forming yokes to centre front and back skirts. 4 The panel inset must now be extended for pleats. Cut up pleats and extend 1 in. for each knife pleat. Double the pleat extension between C and D for inverted pleat on the side seam.

SIDE PLEATS

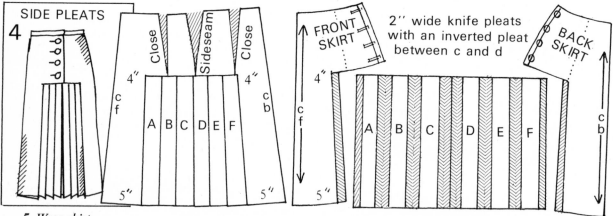

5 *Wrap skirt*
1 Draw whole front of skirt, marking centre front with a dotted line. 2 Draw in skirt wrap, extending it to the waist dart on left side of skirt. Mark buttons and buttonholes. 3 Place draft over another sheet of paper, and trace through skirt section A. 4 Cut out section B which is the normal half front. 5 Section A should be faced as far as the centre front, or this amount can be allowed extra on the draft to turn under.

WRAP SKIRT

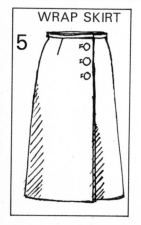

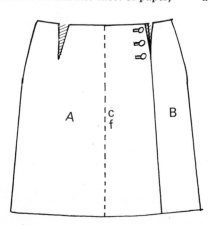

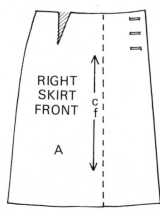

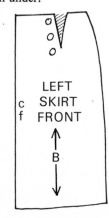

6 *Draped yoke*

1 Draw round skirt front indicating yoke as illustrated. Mark in placement of buttons. 2 Cut away yoke forming 2 sections A and B. 3 Cut along line D to point of dart and close waist dart. 4 Place over fresh paper and re-draw yoke with pleat allowance. The centre front will now be on the bias, but it is better to lay this to the straight grain when cutting out allowing the pleat and side seam of yoke to come on the bias. 5 Re-draw section B making whole front skirt as illustrated.

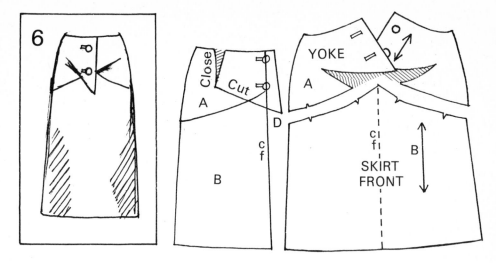

Gored skirts

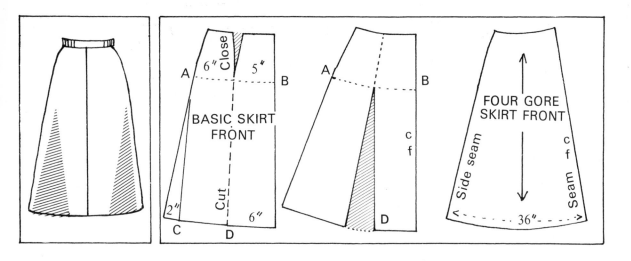

Four gore skirt These three skirts have minimum flare. The final 4 gore skirt above can be used as a block to obtain 6 gore or even 8 gore skirts. Gored skirts do not have darts at the waist, these being into fullness at the hem.

1 Draw round basic skirt block. 2 Mark in hip line 6 in. down from the waist. 3 Extend waist dart to hip line. 4 Add 2 in. extra width to the hem at C and rule new side seam. 5 Rule a dotted line from point of dart

to D parallel to centre front. 6 Cut out skirt, then close waist dart and cut up dotted line from D to point of dart. This will give about 4 in. extra width to the hem. 7 Re-draw on fresh paper for final pattern. 8 Mark straight grain line with arrow up the centre of the panel. When cutting out the panel seams will lie on the bias grain of the fabric giving a soft flare to the skirt. Treat the back in the same way.

Six gore skirt
1 Using the 4 gore skirt as a block, place centre front vertical and draw round. 2 Divide into 2 equal panels A and B bearing in mind that B is only half a panel. Make B 3½ in. wide on hip line, and 6 in. wide at hem. 3 Cut out panels separately. 4 Mark in straight grain up the centre of panel A. In panel B the straight grain will be on the centre frontline. When cutting out, either make a whole panel of B or lay centre line of B against the fold of the material. If the fabric has no pile the gores can be dovetailed in for economical yardage.

Six gore skirt with slot pocket This skirt is cut as above, but has the addition of slot pockets inserted into the front panel seams.
1 Draw round gore skirt block and mark in panels A and B. 2 Mark point D 6 in. from C and draw in pocket welt and pocket as illustrated. 3 Trace through section A including the pocket and cut out. 4 Mark straight grain line up centre of panel. 5 Cut out panel B and mark grain line parallel to centre front. 6 For top pocket, trace through the pocket and welt again. 7 When making up, the 2 welts after being stitched together and turned are stitched into the panel seam between C and D on panel B, together with the top pocket.

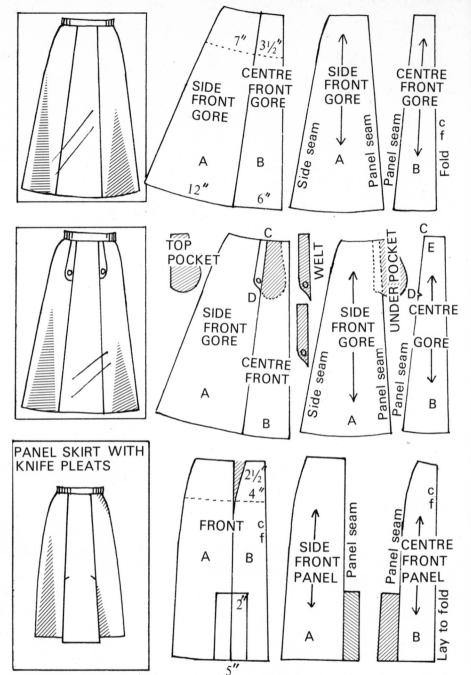

PANEL SKIRT WITH KNIFE PLEATS

Panel skirt with knife pleats
1 Move dart forward to 2½ in. from centre front. 2 Rule in panel seam line from dart point making centre front panel 5 in. wide at the hem. 3 Add knife pleat, making it 8 in. long and 2 in. wide, add pleat each side of panel seam. 4 Lay over fresh paper and trace off section A including pleat and cut out. 5 Cut out centre front panel including pleat. When the panel seam is joined together, the knife pleat should be pressed inwards towards the centre front.

Panel skirt with fan pleat inset As a variation, a pleated godet can be inserted into the seam forming a kick pleat. The fan pleat inset should be about 5 in. tall and shaped like a fan with about 5 knife pleats radiating from the top as illustrated. Pleat this inset after you have stitched the hem, then stitch across the top of the pleats to hold before inserting into the panel seam at D. This is only suitable for light weight woollens and worsted fabrics.

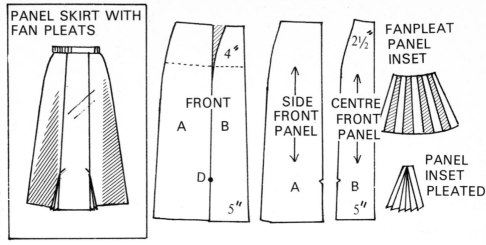

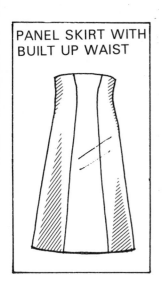

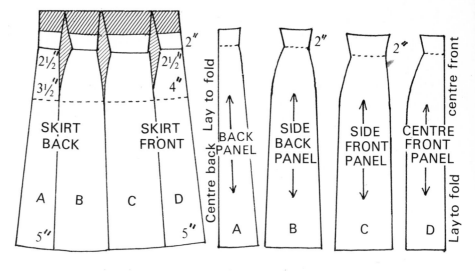

Panel skirt with built-up waist The built-up waist is obtained by placing the bodice blocks over the skirt blocks and shifting the darts to join those of the skirt.

1 Place skirt blocks together, joining along side seam. 2 Place bodice blocks over skirt joining at waist as illustrated. 3 Move skirt darts to 2½ in. from both centre front and centre back seams. 4 Move bodice darts to correspond with skirt darts as illustrated, and draw in built-up waist making it 2 in. deep. 5 Draw in panel seam lines making centre front panel 5 in. wide at the hem, and 4 in. wide on the hip line. Make centre back panel 3½ in. wide on hip line. 6 Cut out panel seam lines from hem to top of fitted waist ignoring darts. The centre front and back panels should be laid against the fold when cutting out. As the built-up waist is sometimes inclined to roll when worn by certain types of figures, it is necessary to insert boning into the seams from waist upwards when making-up. This will keep the built-up waist nicely in position.

65

Fluted panel seamed skirt
1 Draw round skirt block. 2 Move dart towards centre front so that the point is 4 in. from centre front. 3 Draw in front panel, making it 5 in. wide at the hem. 4 Draw in 2 in. flare on to side seam and panel seam as illustrated. Graduate flare into panel seam about 10 in. up from the hem. This flare must be added on to each side of the panel seam. 5 Lay over fresh paper, and trace through panel A and cut out ignoring dart. 6 Cut out front panel without waist dart. When the panel seams are joined together, the hem will flute out as illustrated.

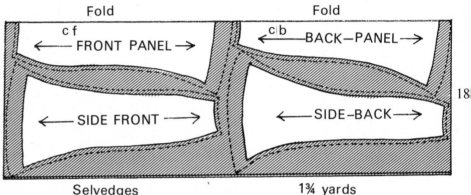

Panel seam with hip drapery The principle of cutting this skirt is the same as above.

1 After having drawn in the panel seam, draw in the curved lines of the hip drapery, and letter the spaces between. 2 Trace through side panel including drapery on to fresh paper and cut out. 3 Cut along lines of drapery, from panel seam line to side seam, and swing each section open about 2 in. Re-draw on fresh paper, carefully marking in the drapery folds and cut out. When the drapery is pleated in correctly it will look soft and fluid being cut on the bias of the fabric. This is an example showing how drapery can be cut on a curved line to fit round the form.

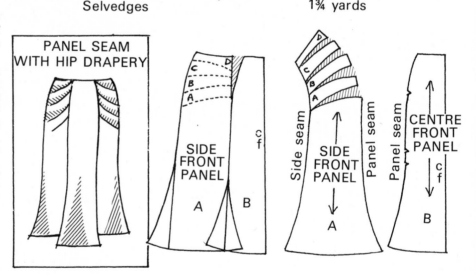

Flounced hem

1 Place front and back skirts together joining along the side seam. 2 Reduce waist 1 in. at centre back, and add 1 in. flare to hem. Connect A to B forming new centre back seam. 3 Draw in flounce making it 8 in. deep in centre front and 12 in. deep at centre back as illustrated. 4 Separate flounce from skirt, and divide into 6 equal sections. 5 Slash up division lines from here to seam line, and open each section about 4 in. to flare. Place over fresh paper and re-draw. The flounce is now semicircular; when cutting out lay centre front to the fold of the fabric.

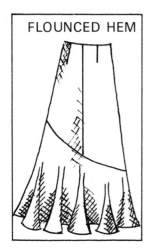

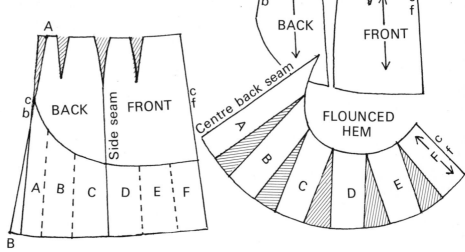

Skirt with trouser pleats

This skirt fits at the waist with 2 little trouser pleats fitting into a waist band 2½ in. deep.

1 Draw round skirt block, marking A 2½ in. from dart and draw pleat line as shown the same length as the dart. 2 Draw in dotted line, continuing pleat line with a graceful curve terminating at B on side seam. B should be about 12 in. from D. 3 Cut out skirt, and slash down from A to B and open 2 in. on the waist. 4 Redraw on fresh paper, marking in the pleat, and turning the dart into a similar pleat. 5 Construct waist band on base of bodice block—pin in the dart and re-draw. Waist band will now be fitted without any darts.

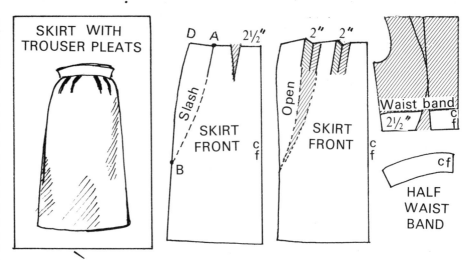

Peg top skirt The peg top skirt is in direct contrast to the flared skirt, as the widest part is across the hips, and the side seams taper to a narrow hem.

1 Draw round skirt block adding 5 in. for inverted pleat in centre front. 2 Turn waist dart into pleat. 3 Draw pocket, extending it 1 in. beyond side seam, and taper side seam in 1 in. at hem. 4 Draw under-pocket (indicated by dotted lines) and trace through section B together with underpocket. 5 Cut out section A then slash through centre of top pocket down to hem line and open pocket $2\frac{1}{2}$ in. as illustrated. 6 Re-draw skirt front and cut lining for top pocket.

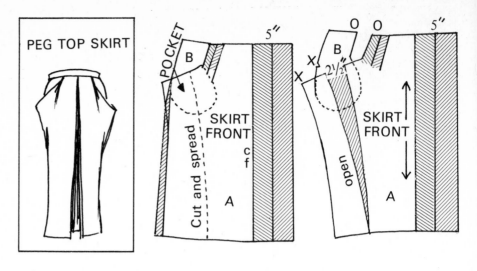

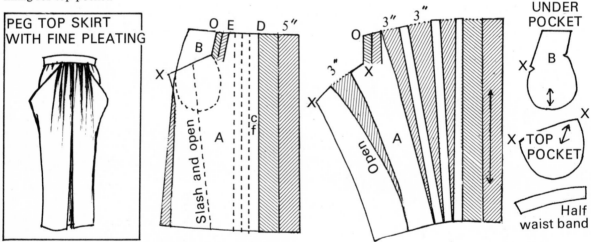

Peg top skirt with fine pleating This skirt is similar to above style, but in addition to an inverted pleat, it has fine pleating in the centre front between the 2 pockets. It should therefore only be made up in a very fine weave or light weight fabric.

1 Proceed in exactly the same method as for cutting the peg top skirt. 2 Slash through the pocket and extend it this time 3 in. 3 Rule 3 dotted lines from waist to hem between D and E. 4 Slash down these lines from waist, and open each 3 in. for pleating as illustrated. 5 Place over fresh paper and re-draw. 6 Draw in top pocket lining and cut out separately.

This pattern clearly shows the concave curve of the hem line which is the complete opposite of the flared or circular skirt. The big pockets help to emphasize

the peg top silhouette.
Panel skirt with central pleating This skirt has fullness at the waist, disappearing at the hem line, similar to the peg top style, but here it is slim over the hips.
1 Draw round skirt block, placing dart $2\frac{1}{2}$ in. from centre front. 2 Widen hem line 1 in. on side seam. 3 Draw in pocket and pocket welt against dart. 4 Draw in centre front panel, then divide panel into 4 equal sections. 5 Trace through pocket and welt and cut out. 6 Cut away front panel without the dart. 7 Slash down division lines from waist to hem, and swing open to enlarge waist for gathering. The hem will remain the same width, but takes on a concave curve. 8 Pin front panel on to fresh paper and re-draw for final pattern.

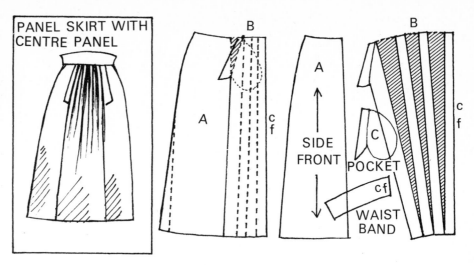

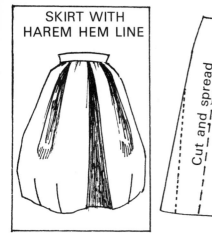

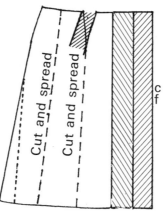

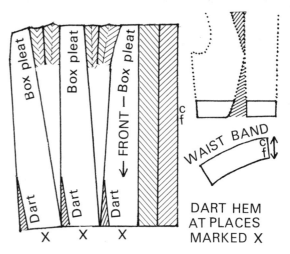

Skirt with harem hem line This is an extreme line, and when in fashion is only suitable for late day wear.
1 Draw round skirt block adding 5 in. to centre front for inverted pleat. 2 Draw in inverted pleat, and widen hem line 2 in. on side seam. 3 Draw in dotted lines as illustrated. 4 Cut out, and slash down dotted lines from waist to hem and open to form 2 wide box pleats. 5 For harem line, the hem must be darted at regular intervals. 6 Construct the waist band on bodice block and cut out without the dart as illustrated.

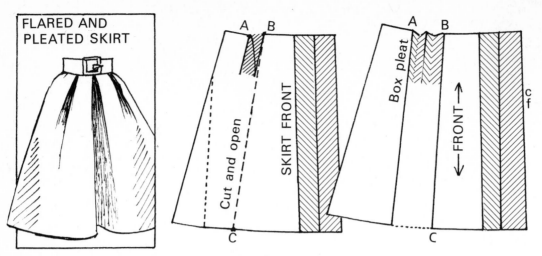

FLARED AND PLEATED SKIRT

Flared and pleated skirt This skirt has unpressed box pleats giving a soft effect. The skirt is first slightly flared; it is then cut up the centre and extended 6 in. as shown for the short unpressed box pleat. Notice the hem line is now part of a circle. When the unpressed pleats are pleated, the skirt will have this bell like effect.

Flared and gathered flounce
This flared skirt has a flared and gathered flounce added to the hem line.
1 Straighten side seam. 2 Draw in skirt flounce making it 8 in. deep. 3 Rule a dotted line from hem up to point of waist dart as illustrated. 4 Cut out skirt, and cut up dotted line to point of dart. 5 Close dart, flaring skirt about 7 in. If a greater flare is needed, cut right through to waist and swing open wider. 6 Re-draw skirt on fresh paper, then cut away flounce. 7 Divide flounce into 3 equal parts, cut up the division lines and spread out for gathering as illustrated. Re-draw on fresh paper for final pattern.

FLARED AND GATHERED FLOUNCE

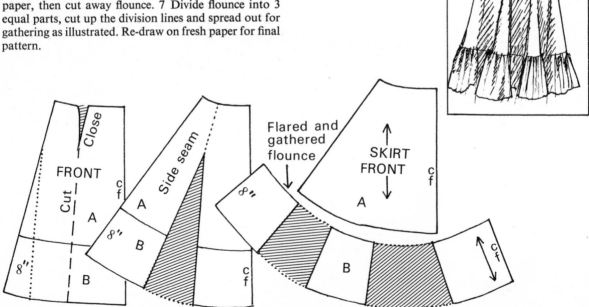

WATERFALL DRAPERY

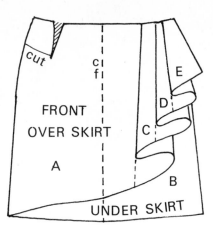

FRONT OVER SKIRT

A

cut

c f

E

D

C

B

UNDER SKIRT

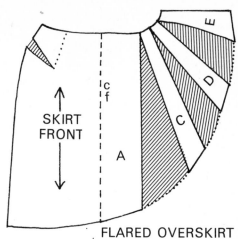

SKIRT FRONT

c f

A

C

D

E

FLARED OVERSKIRT

Waterfall drapery This style has an apron front over skirt falling in waterfall drapery on the left side, and the right dart is moved from the waist to the hip.
1 Place skirt blocks together and draw the whole front. 2 Move R dart to hip as illustrated. 3 Draw carefully the folds of the drapery, numbering each fold C, D, E. 4 Cut up the division lines from hem to waist and open each about 6 in. 5 Pin this carefully on to another sheet of paper and re-draw for final pattern. For underskirt B draw round block pattern of whole skirt front. When making up, skirt A, with the drapery faced and tacked in position, is placed over skirt B, and joined together along waist and side seams.

HIPSTER MINI SKIRT

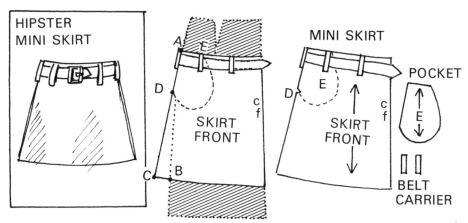

A

E

D

c f

SKIRT FRONT

C B

MINI SKIRT

D

E

SKIRT FRONT

c f

POCKET

E

BELT CARRIER

Hipster mini skirt The hipster skirt hangs from the hips and not from the waist, and is very short ending about 5 in. above the knee.
1 Draw round skirt block. 2 Mark A 4 in. down from the waist and draw in skirt waist round hip. 3 Mark B 16 in. from A and draw in hem line extending from B 2 in. to C. 4 Connect C to A forming side seam. 5 Draw in pocket making D $4\frac{1}{2}$ in. from A and E $2\frac{1}{2}$–3 in. from A. 6 Trace through pocket and cut out. 7 Cut out skirt and draw in belt slots. Make slots 2 in. deep.

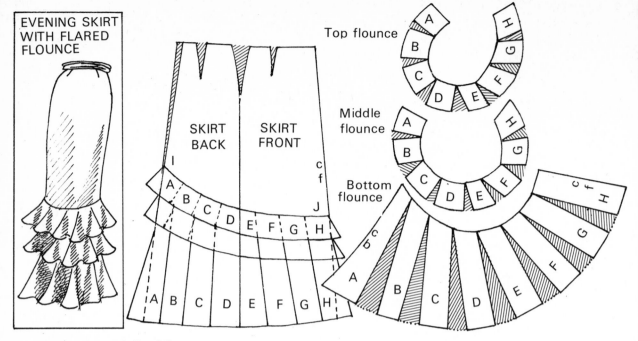

Evening skirt with flared flounce

1 Place front and back skirt blocks together joining along side seam. 2 For evening skirt, lengthen blocks to 36 in. or required length. 3 Reduce waist 1 in. at centre back, rule new back seam down to hem. 4 Draw in the 2 flounces making point I about 16 in. down from the waist, and J about 22 in. from front waist. 5 Flare hem line about 2 in. on centre front and back lines as illustrated. 6 Divide lower skirt into 8 equal sections as illustrated and letter these. 7 Trace off lower skirt which should extend up to just above the lower edge of the top flounce, and slash up division lines from the hem; open to flare as illustrated. 8 Place over fresh paper and re-draw for final pattern. 9 Trace off the 2 short flounces and treat in the same manner flaring to form $\frac{1}{2}$ or $\frac{3}{4}$ circles. When these are stitched to the skirt they will flute out as illustrated.

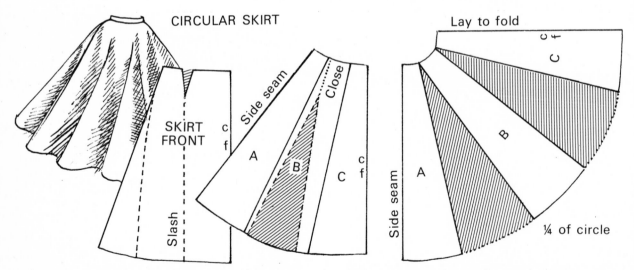

CIRCULAR SKIRT

Circular skirt In the full circular skirt, the half skirt front comprises a $\frac{1}{4}$ of a circle.

1 Straighten side seam as illustrated. 2 Fold in waist dart and slash from hem up to point of dart; this will give a semi-flared skirt. 3 Place over fresh paper and re-draw. 4 Divide skirt into 3 equal sections and label each A, B, C. 5 To make full circle, cut up the division lines from the hem and open wide so that the centre front line lies at right angles to the side seam. This will give a full circular skirt.

Collars

Collars form a background for the face, and are therefore an important feature in pattern cutting, and where possible should form an integral part of the garment. The principle of collar drafting is based upon the relationship between the neck curve and the neck line of the collar. When the two curves are identical, the collar will lie absolutely flat as in the *flat collar*. If the curve of the collar is greater than the neck edge of the dress, the collar will flute as shown in the *fluted collar*. If the collar is straight or given a convex curve, it will stand up close to the neck as shown in the *mandarin collar*. All collar shaping comes somewhere between these two extremes, and with an understanding of this principle it is possible to cut any type of collar. The *Eton collar* is an example of adapting the flat collar, the snipping along the outer edge when overlapped gives a straighter line to the collar, which when it is attached to the neck edge of the dress causes the collar to rise up a little round the back and over the shoulders. Always cut out the whole collar in paper and pin on a dress stand to judge the line.

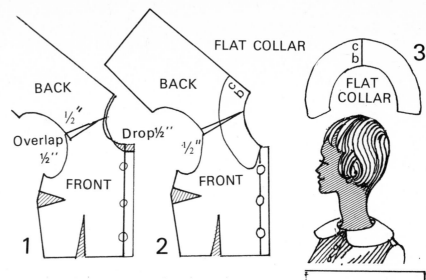

FLAT COLLAR

3

FLAT COLLAR

Flat collar
1 Lay front and back blocks together touching at neck points, but overlapping $\frac{1}{2}$ in. at the armhole. 2 Drop front neck $\frac{1}{2}$ in. but raise neck $\frac{1}{8}$ in. at centre back and at shoulder line. 3 Draw neck curve as shown. 4 Draw in collar making it 2½–3 in. broad keeping it the same width all the way round. The collar terminates at the centre front of the bodice. Trace through as a whole collar for final pattern.

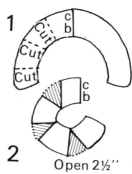

FLUTED COLLAR

Mandarin collar In order to stand up close to the neck, the collar is cut with a slight convex curve. A straight piece of material when joined to the neck will stand up, but it will also stand away from the neck in an ugly fashion. To obtain the desired neat fit, the straight band should be cut from top to bottom in 2 places between the centre front and the shoulder line, and overlapped about $\frac{1}{4}$ in. along the top line. This gives a convex curve to the collar as shown in diagram B. This procedure should raise the centre front of the collar 1 in. higher than the centre back.

Fluted collar
1 Using the flat collar as a foundation, draw round half the collar and mark in centre back. 2 Divide collar into 4 sections. 3 Cut along the division lines from outer to inner edge of collar, and open each slash about 2½ in. to flare. 4 Cut out the 2 halves separately, and join up centre back. When the collar is joined to the neck of the dress it will flute out as illustrated.
A more fluted effect can be achieved by joining two complete circles together. Join on straight grain at centre back. Machine stitch hem twice on outer edge for finish.

ETON COLLAR

Eton collar
1 Use the flat collar as a block and draw round half. 2 Divide into 4 sections and cut along division lines from outer to inner edge. 3 Overlap each about ½ in. along outer edge. 4 Re-draw for final pattern. When this is attached to the dress, the collar will stand closer to the neck at the back and sides.

SAILOR COLLAR

Sailor collar Lay front and back blocks together overlapping ½ in. on the shoulder points. Make neck 4 in. deep in centre front and rule from A to neck point. Make back collar 6 in. deep and square out from B to C. Connect C to A with a straight line. Trace on to fresh paper, laying centre back to the fold. Open out for final collar.

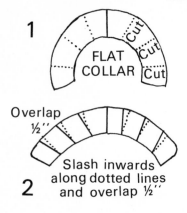

1

FLAT COLLAR

Cut Cut Cut

Overlap ½″

Slash inwards along dotted lines and overlap ½″

2

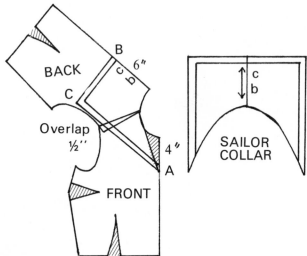

BACK

B

c
b

6″

C

Overlap ½″

4″

A

FRONT

c
b

SAILOR COLLAR

Bertha collar The bertha collar is cut by the same method as the flat collar. Drop the neck 3 in. in centre front and 1½ in. at centre back. Make collar 4 in. deep all round marking in shoulder seam. Trace through, and cut out front and back collars separately. When making up, join along shoulder seams.

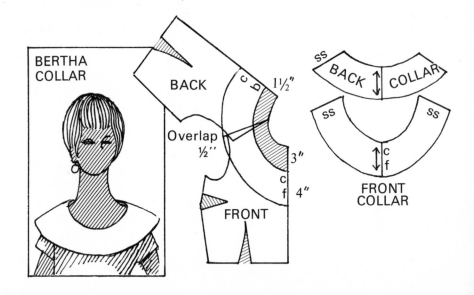

BERTHA COLLAR

BACK

c
b

1½″

Overlap ½″

3″

c
f

4″

FRONT

ss

BACK COLLAR

ss

ss

ss

c
f

FRONT COLLAR

Wing collar The wing collar is cut in a similar way to the mandarin collar, being overlapped along the outer edge to help it cling closely to the neck.
1 Lower front neck $\frac{1}{2}$ in. 2 Mark A $\frac{1}{2}$ in. from neck point. 3 Rule a line from E passing through A to B. This is half neck measure. 4 Square out E to D $3\frac{1}{2}$ in. and B to C 1 in. 5 Connect D to C with a curved line as illustrated. 6 Trace off collar and cut out as whole collar. 7 Mark in 2 dotted lines $1\frac{1}{2}$ in. from centre front and 1 in. apart. 8 Cut up dotted lines from outer edge and overlap $\frac{1}{4}$ in. This will raise the centre front 1 in. higher than centre back.

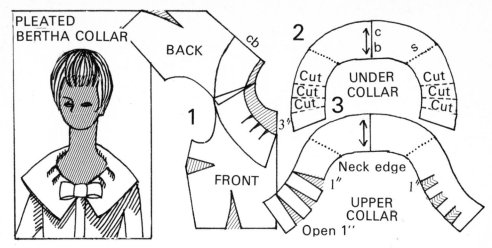

PLEATED BERTHA COLLAR

Pleated bertha collar This is a variation of the bertha collar. To obtain the line illustrated the back is cut with a straighter line to give a slight stand, whereas the front drops 3 in. to give a flattening effect.
1 Construct as for bertha collar. Lower front neck 3 in. and back only $1\frac{1}{2}$ in. 2 Draw in collar making it about 4 in. deep. 3 Mark in pleats 1 in. apart in front collar. 4 Trace through, and cut out whole collar. This will be the under collar. 5 Re-cut, and slash up the pleat lines from neck edge to outer edge, and open each about 1 in. 6 Lay over fresh paper and re-draw marking in the pleats.

To make up, first pleat the neck edge of upper collar before laying over under collar to stitch.

Face framing roll collar
1 Lay front blocks together joining up centre front. 2 Mark A 4 in. down from neck and B $2\frac{1}{2}$ in. along shoulder line. 3 Draw neck curve from B through A continuing on to point of dart as illustrated. 4 Draw back neck curve on back block making C 1 in. down, and D $2\frac{1}{2}$ in. from neck point. 5 Trace back neck curve, and join it to front neck laying D to B. 6 Square out C to E about 5 in. 7 Extend shoulder line from B to F $4\frac{3}{4}$ in. 8 Connect E to F and continue on to point of dart completing collar. Trace collar through on to fresh paper for final pattern and cut out as a whole collar as illustrated.

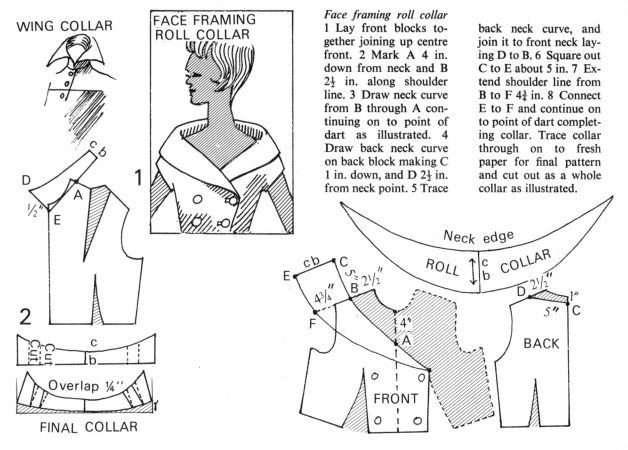

WING COLLAR

FACE FRAMING ROLL COLLAR

FINAL COLLAR

Rever Revers are cut in 1 piece with the bodice. 1 Add ¾ in. button wrap up centre front. 2 Mark B 6 in. down from A. 3 Rule rolling line from D to B. 4 Rule a horizontal line from B to C 7½ in. in length. 5 Rule a line connecting C to D. 6 Trace rever BCD and cut out. 7 Lay reversed tracing against neck point rolling lines together and re-draw.

REVER

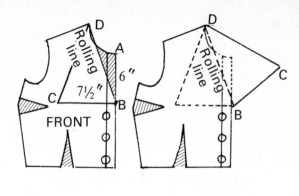

Roll collar The roll collar combines the rever and collar in 1 piece with the bodice. 1 Lay back and front blocks together overlapping shoulder points ½ in. Add 1 in. button wrap. 2 Mark B 6 in. down from A and rule a line to D. 3 Draw in rever on bodice making B to C 5½ in. and D to E 3 in. 4 Draw round normal neck for back collar, making it 3 in. deep at centre back. Connect E to F following back neck curve. 5 The rever and collar must now be traced and reversed laying rolling lines together as shown in the diagram. 6 Cut the facing in the usual way. To avoid a join up centre back, lay the 2 facings together joining up centre back as shown in diagram 3. The facing will now become the upper collar. Diagram 4 shows how to obtain a closer fit at the back of the collar by simply straightening the back neck curve as illustrated.

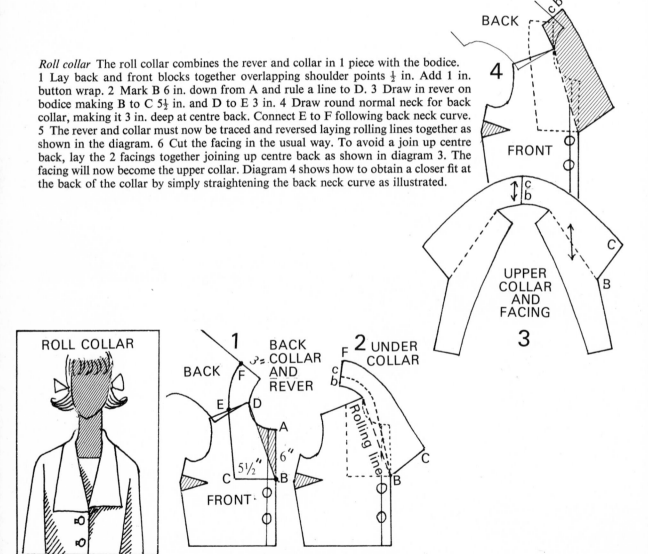

ROLL COLLAR

BLOUSE ROLL COLLAR 1

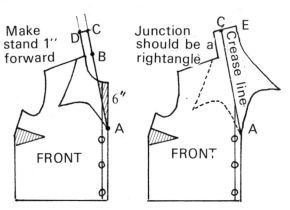

Make stand 1'' forward

Junction should be a rightangle

Crease line

6''

FRONT

FRONT

Blouse Roll Collar 1 This collar has a 1 in. stand and 2 in. fall. In order for a high close fit at the back, the junction of the neck point and back neck line should be a right angle.
1 Mark A 6 in. down from neck on button wrap 1 in. wide. 2 Rule crease line from A through B which is 1 in. forward from neck point, on to C. B to C is half back neck measure. 3 Square out at C 1 in. to D, and connect to neck point. This is the collar stand. 4 Draw in rever on bodice. 5 Trace rever and reverse, laying crease lines together, and draw round. 6 Square out C to E 2 in. and connect E to rever completing collar.

Straight collar This is the simplest of all collars, comprising a straight band about 2 in. wide which is stitched to the normal neck line which is lowered ½ in. in centre front. The crease line should be drawn from the neck point to D about 5 in. down. The neck is worn open as illustrated. The draft shown here is for only half the collar. Lay centre back to fold when cutting out.

STRAIGHT COLLAR 2

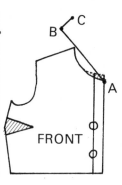

FRONT

HALF COLLAR

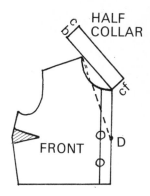

FRONT

Roll collar 3 If the collar is required to lie flat at the back, the back neck should be drafted with a concave curve.
1 Mark A 1½ in. forward from centre front, and level with top of waist dart. 2 Mark B and C as previously and draw in crease line. 3 Square out from C 1 in. back to D and rule construction line to neck point. 4 Draw concave curve from B to D. 5 Square out line BD 1 in. to E. 6 Connect E with concave curve to neck point. 7 Draw in rever, and reverse laying crease lines together. 8 Extend centre back line from D, then connect outer edge of collar to centre back as illustrated.

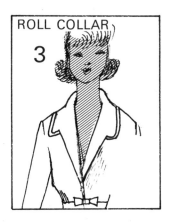

ROLL COLLAR 3

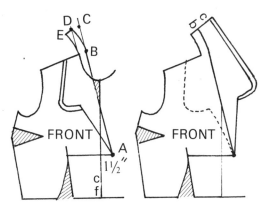

FRONT

FRONT

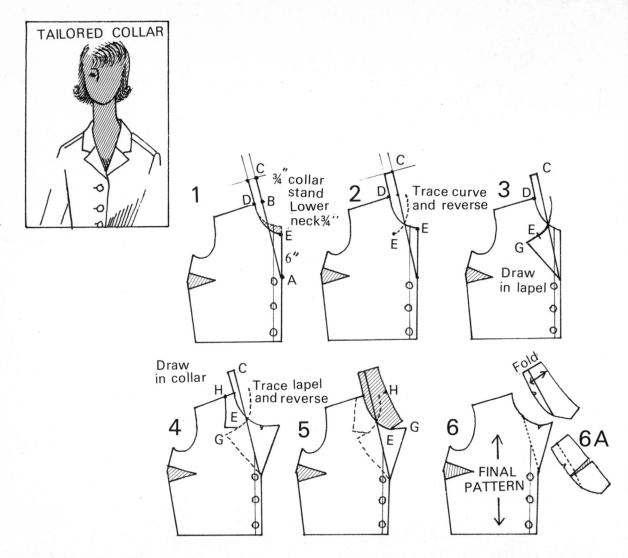

TAILORED COLLAR

1 ¾" collar stand Lower neck ¾" 6"

2 Trace curve and reverse

3 Draw in lapel

4 Draw in collar / Trace lapel and reverse

5

6 FINAL PATTERN

6A Fold

Tailored collar This is constructed on similar lines to the roll collar, the difference being that the tailored collar is composed of two parts, A the back collar and B the lapel.

1 Add ¾ in. button wrap down centre front, and lower neck ¾ in. 2 Mark point B ¾ in. forward from D. 3 Rule crease line from A through B and on to C which is half back neck measure from B. 4 Square out at C ¾ in. back, and connect with straight line to D. This forms the collar

stand. 5 Trace front neck curve from D to E including crease line; turn tracing over and reverse laying crease lines together, and retrace neck curve as shown by dotted line in diagram 2. 6 Draw in lapel extending E to G 1½ in. and connect to A. 7 Trace lapel and reverse as shown in diagram 4. Mark point E with a balance mark. 8 Draw in collar against bodice, making H 1½ in. from neck point, and I 1½ in. from E as shown. 9 Trace collar and reverse. 10 Square out at

centre back then connect H to centre back line. The collar is now complete, it should measure 2¼ in. deep at centre back having ¾ in. stand, and 1½ in. fall. 11 Cut out the collar separating it from the bodice and lapel. If a wider collar is drafted, it will be necessary to slash through the collar on the outer edge and open ½ in. for ease over the shoulder muscle. See diagram 6A.

The back neck line can be cut with a slightly curved line instead of

straight if the collar is required to lie flatter at the back. When making up for a suit, the under collar is cut in wool and on the true bias; but the top collar in tweed will be cut with the centre back on the straight grain of the fabric. When making up in silk, rayon, or cotton, both upper and under collar may be cut with centre back on the straight grain, but the collar must be slashed on the outer edge and opened ½ in. to avoid dragging.

BUILT-UP NECKLINE

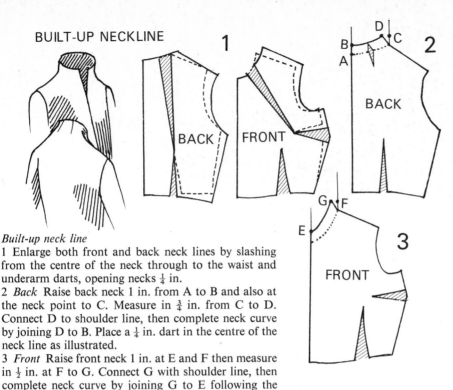

BACK

FRONT

BACK

FRONT

Built-up neck line

1 Enlarge both front and back neck lines by slashing from the centre of the neck through to the waist and underarm darts, opening necks ¼ in.

2 *Back* Raise back neck 1 in. from A to B and also at the neck point to C. Measure in ¾ in. from C to D. Connect D to shoulder line, then complete neck curve by joining D to B. Place a ¼ in. dart in the centre of the neck line as illustrated.

3 *Front* Raise front neck 1 in. at E and F then measure in ½ in. at F to G. Connect G with shoulder line, then complete neck curve by joining G to E following the neck curve.

Soft tailored collar

1 Widen neck ½ in. on shoulder, and drop 1 in. at centre front. 2 Add 1 in. button wrap. 3 Mark C 6 in. down from B and D 1 in. in from new neck point. 4 Rule crease line from C passing through D to E. Make D to E half back neck measure. 5 Square out at E 1 in. to F. 6 Connect with a curved line to D. 7 Square out line DF, 1 in. to H, connect H to neck point. 8 Trace front neck curve and reverse as shown in diagram 2. 9 Draw in collar and lapel joining at B. Make collar 3 in. wide on shoulder. 10 Trace collar and lapel and reverse as shown in diagram 4. 11 Draw in centre back line of collar making F to G 3 in. Connect I to G to complete the collar. 12 Cut out collar and divide into 3 parts. 13 Slash along dividing lines and open each ¾ in. on outer edge. 14 Re-draw for final collar.

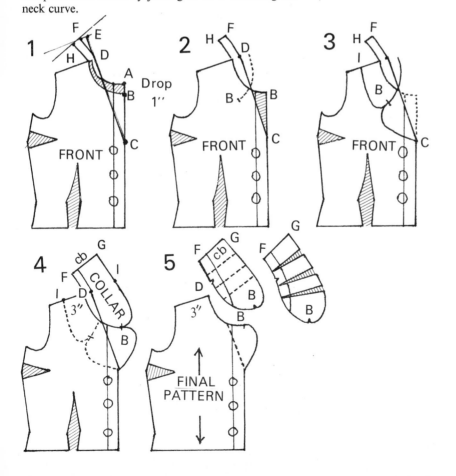

Drop 1″

FRONT

FINAL PATTERN

COLLAR

SOFT TAILOR COLLAR

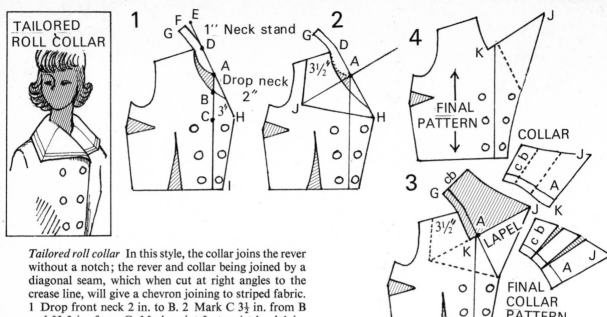

TAILORED ROLL COLLAR

Tailored roll collar In this style, the collar joins the rever without a notch; the rever and collar being joined by a diagonal seam, which when cut at right angles to the crease line, will give a chevron joining to striped fabric. 1 Drop front neck 2 in. to B. 2 Mark C 3½ in. from B and H 3 in. from C. Mark point I at waist level 1 in. from centre front. Rule a line from H through D which is 1 in. in from the neck to E. Make D to E half back neck measure. 3 Square out 1 in. from E to F, and connect F to D with a curved line. 4 Square out 1 in. from line FD to G and connect to neck point. 5 Extend front neck curve from B to crease line and rule a line from H to I. Put in buttons. 6 At A rule a line passing through point A at right angles to the crease line and draw in rever and collar as shown joining at point J. Make collar 3½ in. wide on the shoulder, and A to J 7 in. 7 Trace rever and collar and reverse, joining outer edge of collar to centre back line as shown in diagram 3. 8 Cut away collar, cutting along JK line and KG line leaving the rever joined to the bodice. 9 Slash collar in 2 places along outer edge, and open each ¾ in. Re-draw for final collar.

Shawl collar 1
1 Place front and back blocks together joining along the shoulder line. 2 Add ¾ in. button wrap up centre front and mark point A 7 in. down from neck. 3 Rule rolling line from A to B. 4 Draw in collar, making it 6 in. deep at centre back and on the shoulders and coming to a point at A. 5 Add ⅛ in. ease at C on centre back. 6 Trace collar, and reverse tracing; lay rolling lines together and draw round. This completes the under collar which is cut in 1 piece with the bodice front. 7 The facing or top collar must now be cut by drawing round the outer edge of the collar, down centre front and along about 2½ in. of shoulder line. This is cut out separately with the centre back placed to the fold of the fabric.

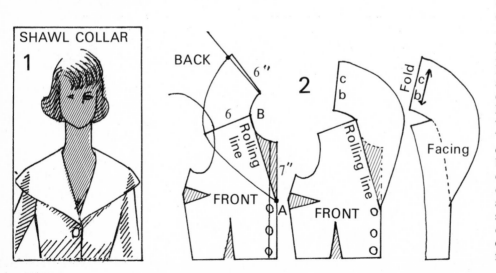

SHAWL COLLAR

Shawl collar 2 This can be adapted from shawl collar 1.

1 Draw round pattern of shawl collar. 2 Draw in rolling line making A 1½ in. from neck point. From A draw curve line round back neck line forming collar stand. 3 At B add 1½ in. and graduate to nothing at C. 4 In order to make the collar stand up at the back, it is necessary to slash the back collar in 3 places and overlap each about ¾ in. as shown. This will automatically straighten the back neckline, which will help the collar to fit closer to the neck. The collar stand may be stiffened by interlining if desired. Cut the top collar by drawing round the pattern like a facing, but the centre back must be placed to the fold.

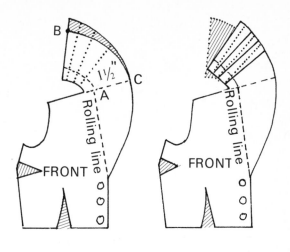

Shawl collar 3 This collar has a shoulder seam, which can be shaped to give the graceful line illustrated.

1 Place both front blocks together, joining along centre front line, and draw round marking in a double breasted fastening. 2 Draw rolling line from top button to B which is 1 in. forward from the neck point. 3 Rule a line from B to C 7 in. then draw in rever and front lapel. 4 Lay back block against front, placing back neck point to B, with shoulder lines touching. 5 Draw in back collar as illustrated. 6 Trace collar and rever, then reverse laying rolling lines together, and draw round as shown in diagram. 7 Cut along collar shoulder seam from C to B separating it from the rever. 8 Divide the back collar into 3, then cut up division lines from outer edge, and overlap each ¾ in. 9 Re-draw collar as a whole collar, and hollow out shoulder seams as illustrated.

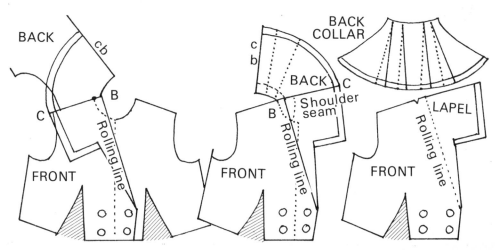

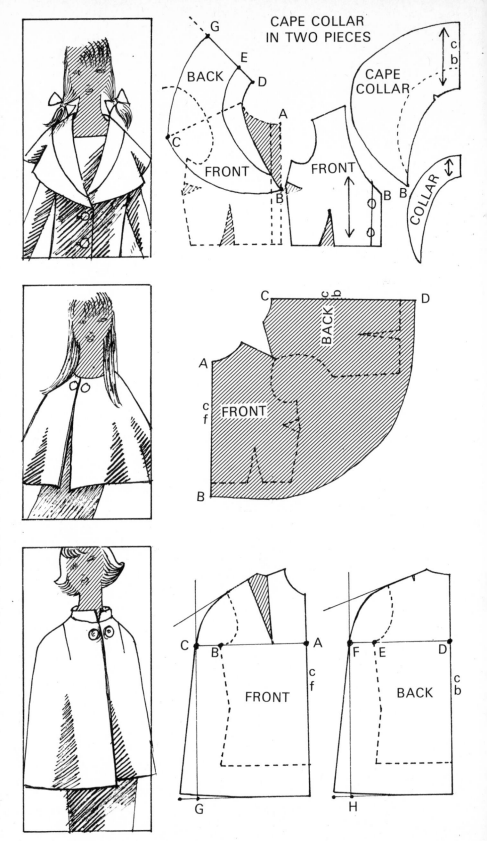

Cape collar The draft for this is similar to the flat collar.

1 Place front and back blocks together joining along the shoulder line. Add 1 in. button extension. 2 A to B is 8 in. Draw in neck line. 3 Extend shoulder line 10 in. to C, then draw in roll collar making it $2\frac{1}{2}$ in. wide at centre back and graduating to a point at centre front. 4 Draw in cape collar from B to G which is $7\frac{1}{2}$ in. from D. Cut out and make up the 2 collars separately.

Circular cape The full circular cape is obtained by placing the bodice front and back blocks to form a right angle, with shoulder points just touching and forming a large dart. There is no side seam.

1 Lay blocks as illustrated. 2 Make AB and CD required length. 3 Connect B to D with a semicircular curve. Centre front and back must be cut on the straight grain of the fabric.

Straight cape with side seams This fits best with a shoulder dart, but it can be moved to the neck opening if desired.

1 Draw round bodice blocks. 2 Draw horizontal lines across bodice passing through base of armhole. 3 Extend B to C $\frac{1}{4}$ of AB measure. Extend E to F same as B to C. 4 Square out at C and F and prolong shoulder line to intersect. 5 Draw shoulder curve as illustrated through C and F and continuing on to hem, which should terminate about 2 in. further out from G and H. CB measurement should never be less than $\frac{1}{4}$ of A to B.

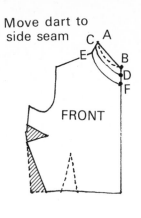

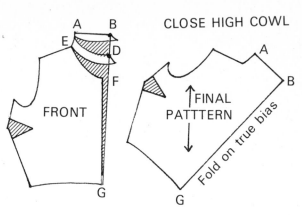

CLOSE HIGH COWL

FINAL PATTERN

Fold on true bias

1 *Close high cowl* As all cowl neck lines cut in 1 piece with the bodice have to be cut out on the true bias of the fabric, the front waist dart should be eliminated.
1 Using block with built-up neck line, draw round bodice eliminating the dart into the side seam. 2 Rule a line from A to B at the neck. 3 Mark points A, B, C, D, E, F all 1 in. apart, and draw in fold curves. 4 Cut out draft and cut along fold lines from D to C and F to E and open as illustrated. Line AB should be at right angles to line BG. 5 Draw in line BG forming new

centre front line. The centre front and the neck line must always be at right angles to each other. Place centre front on true bias when cutting out in fabric.

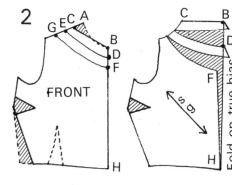

Fold on true bias

2 *High cowl neck with double drape*
1 Using the normal bodice block, mark point C 1 in. from A. 2 Rule a line from C to B. 3 Mark points E and D and F and G, making them all 1 in. apart and draw in fold lines. 4 Cut out bodice eliminating waist dart into side seam. Line CB is now the neck line. 5 Slash along fold lines from D to E and F to G and swing open so that point B forms a right angle to line DH. 6 Square out B to C and B to H forming new centre front line.

4 *Alternative method* This method eliminates both darts into the front neck line.
1 Fold in underarm dart and waist dart points meeting. 2 Slash from centre of neck to point of darts. 3 Lay a tailor's square along centre front to form a right angle with the neck point and draw round.

This method is not so accurate as 2 and 3.

ALTERNATIVE METHOD

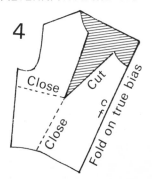

Close Cut
Close
c f
Fold on true bias

DEEP COWL NECK

Move dart to side seam

true bias

3 *Deep cowl neck* This is cut in precisely the same method as in 2.
1 Draw round bodice front. 2 Mark B 5 in. down centre front from neck point, and rule a line to point A. 3 Cut out bodice, transferring waist dart into side seam. 4 Draw in cowl fold lines making points C and E and D and F all 2 in. apart. 5 Slash up fold lines from D to C and F to E and swing up B to form a right angle to A and G. 6 Square out B to A and B to G as illustrated. Check that line AB is exactly the same length as AB on the original draft; in this case it is 8 in. 7 Swing up point D until it touches line BG and draw round this section which will indicate where the second drape is located.

Making the dress block

To construct the dress block, first draw round the bodice block, then lay the basic skirt block against it joining the waist so that the centre front is vertical. Disregard the overlap of waists at side seam. Hip line and waist line should be horizontal. Draw round bodice and skirt forming dress block. Connect A to hip line as illustrated for fitted line.

Mini shift dress 1

1 Draw round one-piece dress block. 2 Make side seam easy fitting by connecting A to C with a straight line. Ignore waist dart. 3 Widen neck 1½ in. at D. 4 Transfer shoulder dart to side seam, making B about 6 in. down from A. 5 Fold in shoulder dart, and cut from B to point of dart. 6 Place over fresh paper and re-draw for final pattern.

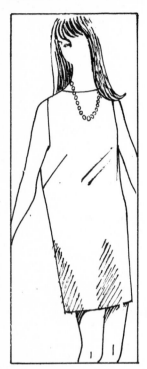

DRESS BLOCK AND MINI SHIFT DRESS 1

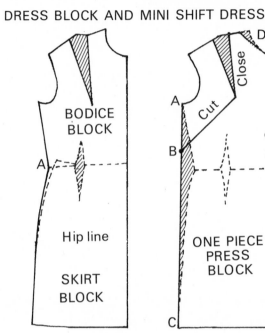

BODICE BLOCK

Hip line

SKIRT BLOCK

ONE PIECE PRESS BLOCK

A Cut Close D

B

c f

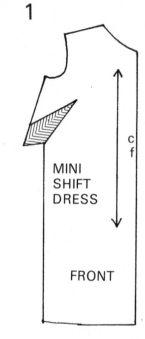

MINI SHIFT DRESS

c f

FRONT

Mini shift dress 2 This is very similar to the shift dress above, but here the dress is divided into 2 sections A and B.

1 Draw round dress block making side seam straight and point D 1 in. out at the hem. 2 Mark B 5 in. down from A, and rule a line from B to the bust dart 1½ in. above dart point. Then square out from here to centre front forming yoke. 3 Widen neck 1 in. at C. 4 Cut away yoke and fold in shoulder dart. Re-draw on fresh paper and mark this A. 5 Cut out skirt section ignoring waist dart.

This simple design looks well made up in a bold striped material when a feature can be made of chevron joining of the stripes on the yoke side seam as illustrated.

MINI SHIFT DRESS 2

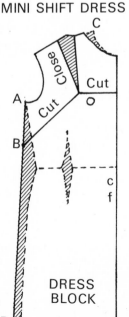

A Cut Close Cut C

B

c f

DRESS BLOCK

D

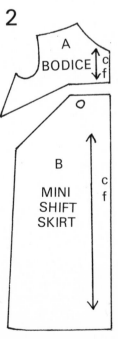

A BODICE

c f

B

MINI SHIFT SKIRT

c f

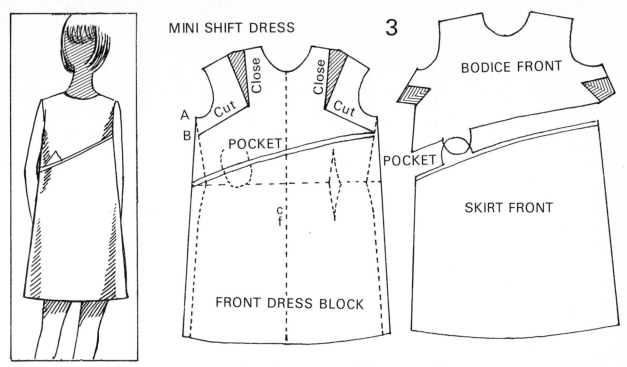

MINI SHIFT DRESS

3

Labels on diagram: Close · Cut · A · B · Close · Cut · POCKET · c f · FRONT DRESS BLOCK · BODICE FRONT · POCKET · SKIRT FRONT

Mini shift dress 3 This dress has an asymmetric bodice, therefore the whole of the dress front must be drafted. 1 Lay dress blocks together joining along centre front, and draw round. 2 Make dress easy fitting by adding 1 in. extra width at the hem line, and straighten the side seam. 3 Transfer shoulder dart to underarm, making B 2½ in. below A. 4 Draw in bodice yoke as illustrated. 5 Cut away bodice from skirt. 6 Lay bodice over fresh paper and re-draw, leaving out waist dart. Trace off skirt with pocket ignoring the waist dart.

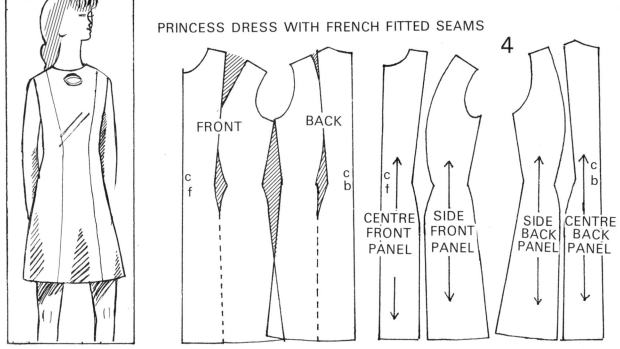

PRINCESS DRESS WITH FRENCH FITTED SEAMS

4

Labels on diagram: FRONT · BACK · c f · c b · CENTRE FRONT PANEL · SIDE FRONT PANEL · SIDE BACK PANEL · CENTRE BACK PANEL

Princess dress with French fitted seams 4 Here the shoulder and waist darts are so placed as to form panel seams running from shoulder to hem. The block is otherwise unaltered. Fitting or letting out for ease being done on the panel seam lines. This design has minimum skirt flare giving a hem about 48 in. wide.

SEMI-FITTED PRINCESS DRESS WITH SHOULDER CAPE

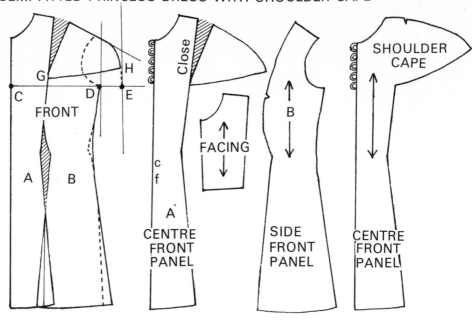

Semi-fitted princess dress with shoulder cape

1 Draw round dress block, arranging darts to form panel seams. 2 Flare hem line by extending 1 in. at hem on either side of construction line, and 1 in. at side seam. 3 Construct shoulder cape by extending D to E ¼ of C to D measure. 4 Square out E with line F. 5 Extend shoulder line to cross line EF. 6 Draw cape shoulder curve as illustrated. 7 Draw in lower edge of cape from G curving up to H which is 2 in. above E. 8 Trace through front side panel B, and cut out. 9 Cut out centre front panel A including the cape. 10 Fold in shoulder dart in panel A, re-draw and cut out for final pattern. 11 Trace front facing round neck line and centre front opening, and along CD line to panel seam and cut out.

FLARED CHEMISE DRESS

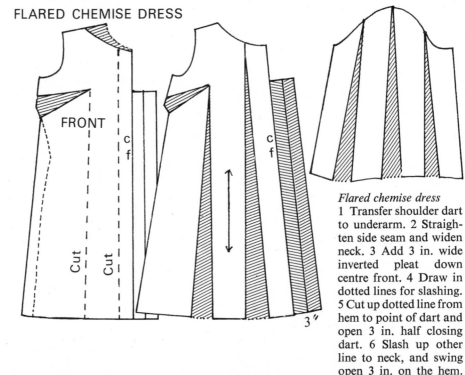

Flared chemise dress

1 Transfer shoulder dart to underarm. 2 Straighten side seam and widen neck. 3 Add 3 in. wide inverted pleat down centre front. 4 Draw in dotted lines for slashing. 5 Cut up dotted line from hem to point of dart and open 3 in. half closing dart. 6 Slash up other line to neck, and swing open 3 in. on the hem. 7 Flare sleeve as shown. Keep pleat on bias grain.

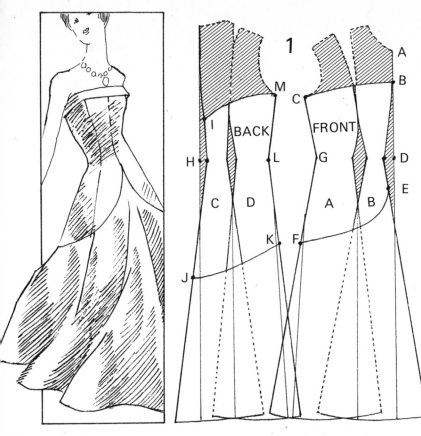

1

Long torso line evening dress with circular skirt This boned evening dress is cut with princess panel seams which are fitted closely to the figure; extra fitting can be taken on each seam if needed. 1 Draw round back and front dress blocks. 2 Draw in panel seams by continuing dart lines to hem line as illustrated. Reduce waist back and front 1 in. 3 Draw in neck line, making A to B 4 in. deep and connect to C with a curved line. 4 Draw in bodice front making point E 4 in. from D and F 11 in. from G. Draw in hip line as shown in the illustration. 5 Draw in bodice on back draft making point I 5 in. up from H. Draw in bodice top with a curved line from I to M. 6 Point J is 15 in. from H, and K 11 in. from L. Draw in back hip line. 7 Label bodice panels A, B, C, D; trace through individual panels on to fresh paper, and cut out.

Back skirt flounce

1 Lay panels C and D together as illustrated joining along panel seam and waists level. The top bodice will overlap but this will not matter. Cut out the back skirt portion ignoring the dotted lines, and slash in 3 places from hem to hip line and open to form a quarter of a circle as illustrated. 2 The front skirt should be treated in the same way. 3 Check that the skirt side seams are the same length before cutting final pattern. The top of the strapless bodice is banded with a piece of fabric cut on the true bias.

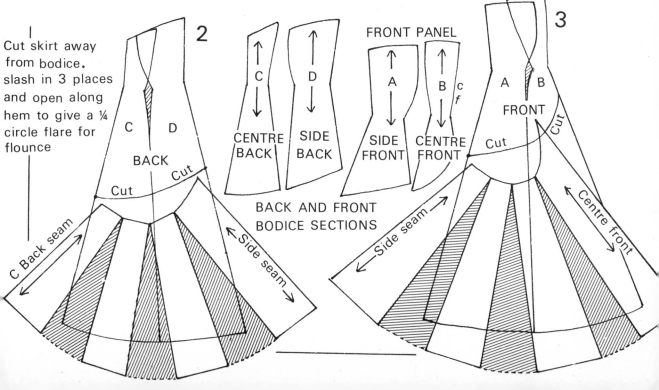

Trouser drafting

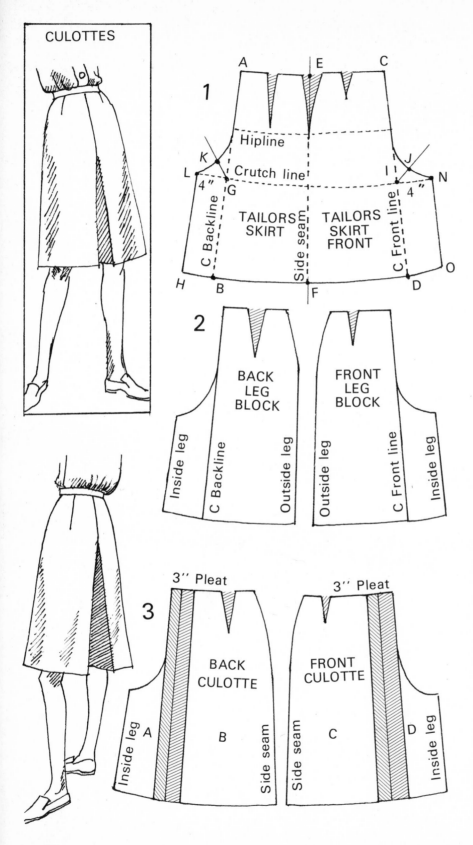

Most trousers can be developed from the skirt block, but in order to draft the leg block, one additional measurement is needed, i.e. *the depth of crutch.* This measurement can be taken by measuring from the waist to chair seat with the client sitting, and adding 1 in. extra for ease. It can also be obtained as a proportion of the hip measurement, thus for 33 in. hips it is 12 in. increasing $\frac{3}{4}$ in. with each 2 in. size increase, therefore for 35 in. hips the crutch depth is $12\frac{3}{4}$ in. and for 37 in. hips it is $13\frac{1}{2}$ in. and so on.

Correct method of taking measurements

Waist	Take snug measure
Hips	8 in. below waist
Crutch depth	From waist to chair seat plus 1 in. ease
Side length	From waist to ankle. The knee is midway between hips and ankle

The leg block
1 Place the tailor's skirt blocks together joining down the side seam. 2 Put crutch line, making point G $13\frac{1}{2}$ in. from A. 3 Extend G to L and I to N $\frac{1}{5}$ of skirt block hip measure = 4 in. 4 Square down from L to H and N to O ruling leg seams parallel to centre front and back lines. 5 Mark H on knee level and draw in hem line parallel to crutch line. 6 For crutch curve, rule a line at 45° through G and I. 7 Mark K 2 in. from G, and J 2 in. from I, then draw in crutch curve from L passing through K, and H passing through J to centre front and back lines about 3in. above crutch line. 8 Cut out draft, then cut up the side seam dividing the pattern into 2

separate pieces: the front leg block, and the back leg block. The side seam now becomes the outside leg seam. To obtain crease line, fold the outside leg seam to the centre front and back line and crease.

Culottes Culottes, giving the appearance of a divided skirt, are a combination of the skirt and trouser, with an inverted pleat added at centre back and front. The leg block can easily be adapted for culottes, by simply adding a 3 in. wide inverted pleat.

1 Cut up centre front and back lines. 2 Place over fresh paper with sections A and D placed 3 in. away from B and C. 3 Redraw round pattern, marking in the 3 in. wide inverted pleat up the centre front and back lines as illustrated.

The length of the culottes can be made as long or as short as desired according to the prevailing fashion.

Basic shorts

Basic shorts Shorts can be cut successfully by adapting the leg block as well as by drafting.

To adapt from the leg block:

1 Draw round the leg block making A to C and B to D 4 in. deep. 2 Draw hem line by connecting C to D with a line parallel to the hip line, i.e. slightly curved. 3 Cut out, and cut up the side seam separating the legs. 4 In order to give a more graceful hang, and a better fit at the back, slash from the hem up to the point of the back dart and pivot to half close the dart. This should give about 2 in. extra girth to the back leg—see diagram 2, 5 Pin over fresh paper. and re-draw back leg in its altered shape and cut out for final pattern. 6 To obtain centre front and back crease line, fold each leg in half placing the centre front and back to the side seam and crease. This will form the crease line.

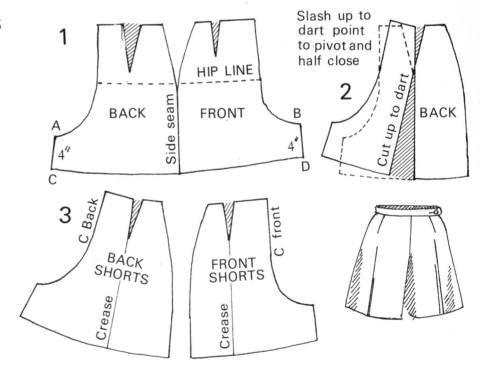

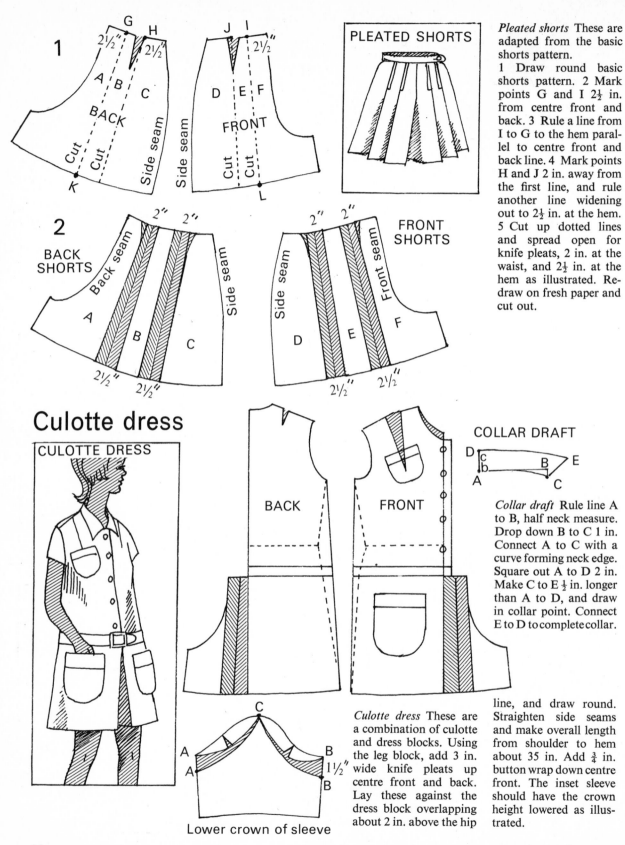

1

2½" G H 2½"

A B C

BACK

Cut Cut Side seam

K

J I

2½"

D E F

FRONT

Side seam Cut Cut

L

PLEATED SHORTS

2

BACK SHORTS

2" 2"

Back seam

A

B C

2½" 2½"

Side seam

FRONT SHORTS

2" 2"

Side seam

D E F

Front seam

2½" 2½"

Pleated shorts These are adapted from the basic shorts pattern.

1 Draw round basic shorts pattern. 2 Mark points G and I 2½ in. from centre front and back. 3 Rule a line from I to G to the hem parallel to centre front and back line. 4 Mark points H and J 2 in. away from the first line, and rule another line widening out to 2½ in. at the hem. 5 Cut up dotted lines and spread open for knife pleats, 2 in. at the waist, and 2½ in. at the hem as illustrated. Redraw on fresh paper and cut out.

Culotte dress

CULOTTE DRESS

BACK FRONT

COLLAR DRAFT

D c B E
b
A C

Collar draft Rule line A to B, half neck measure. Drop down B to C 1 in. Connect A to C with a curve forming neck edge. Square out A to D 2 in. Make C to E ½ in. longer than A to D, and draw in collar point. Connect E to D to complete collar.

C

A B
A 1½" B

Lower crown of sleeve

Culotte dress These are a combination of culotte and dress blocks. Using the leg block, add 3 in. wide knife pleats up centre front and back. Lay these against the dress block overlapping about 2 in. above the hip

line, and draw round. Straighten side seams and make overall length from shoulder to hem about 35 in. Add ¾ in. button wrap down centre front. The inset sleeve should have the crown height lowered as illustrated.

Trouser draft
Front leg

1 Rule line A to B full length 42 in. 2 Square out A to C ¼ waist measurement. 3 Mark point D 7½ in. down from A and square out to L ¼ hip measurement minus ¼ in. 4 Connect L to C continuing on ¾ in. to M. Connect M to A with a curve forming front waist line. 5 To construct fork, mark point E crutch length, e.g. 13½ in. (⅓ hip measurement plus 1 in.). 6 Square out E to F 3¾ in. (1/12 hip measurement plus ½ in.). EG is half EF. 7 Draw in front fork with a curved line from F through G and D to A. 8 For inside leg seam mark point H midway between E and B. This is the knee level. Square out H to J ⅔ of E to F measure. 9 Extend B to K 1½ in. and draw in front inside leg seam from K through J to F. 10 Complete leg by drawing in outside leg seam, these are tapered at the ankle. Drop a vertical line from L to X. From X measure in 2½ in. to N, then connect L to N and complete ankle by ruling a line from N to K.

Back leg

11 F to O is 2 in., J to P is 1¾ in. and K to Q 1½ in. Draw back inside leg seam. 12 For crutch curve, G to U is ¾ in. Point R is midway between F and E. Draw construction line from R through G to S continuing 1¼ in. up to T. Draw back crutch curve from O through U and S to T. 13 T to V is ¼ waist measure plus 1 in. ease. L to W is 1½ in. Draw in back outside leg seam making it parallel to line LN. A dart 1 in. wide is placed in the centre back waist, and a small one ½ in. wide in the front.

The front and back legs are then traced off separately. The shaded part represents the back leg.

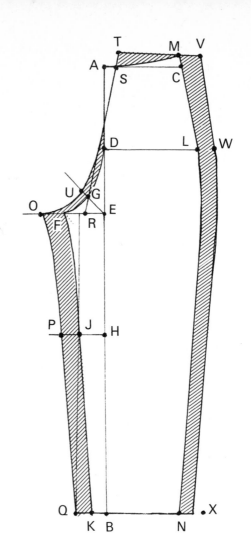

Adapting the bodice block for lingerie

Just as the bodice block needs enlarging for outer wear, it needs to be made smaller for lingerie.

1 Take ½ in. off the side seams. 2 At the armhole, measure in another ½ in. This will give a curve to the top of the side seam. 3 Take off 1 in. at centre back waist and graduate to hip level. 4 The shoulder dart is widened on each side *half the width of the dart.* 5 Mark these points A and B and draw lines to dart point. 6 Check underarm seam length, and adjust at base of armhole if different.

ADAPTING THE BLOCK FOR LINGERIE

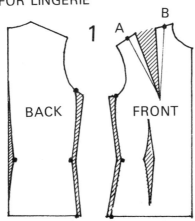

FINAL LINGERIE BLOCK

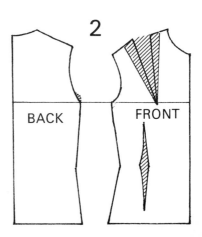

Semi-fitted slip

1 Draw round lingerie block.
2 Continue centre front line and side seam required length and draw in hem line. 3 Draw in bodice yoke making point B 6 in. from A, and C 2½ in. from B. 4 Mark point D 6 in. down from shoulder, and F 6 in. down from E. 5 Mark point G 2 in. down from armhole, and H 3 in. down from G. 6 Draw in style lines. 7 Connect bust point to I with dotted line. 8 Cut away bodice yoke and mark this section A and skirt part B. 9 Close shoulder dart and cut from I up dotted line to bust point, transferring the dart to under the bust. Cut out sections A and B separately.

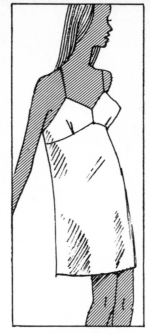

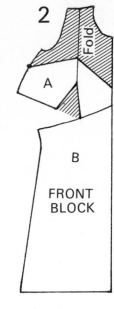

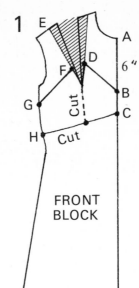

Brassiere cutting

Brassiere 1 For brassiere cutting, the block must be further modified. In addition to the enlarged shoulder dart it must also be reduced to a tighter bust measure.

1 Take in a further ½ in. on the side seam. 2 Mark point A 7 in. down from neck and B and C each 6 in. down from the shoulder. Point D is 2 in. down from E. Draw in style lines. 3 For lower part of brassiere mark points F and G 4 in. up from the waist and connect with a curved line. 4 For tight fit mark bust point 1 in. below dart point and move waist dart immediately below. Prolong to join the bust point. Widen this dart to 1½ in. at base of brassiere. 5 Connect B and C to bust point with curved lines as illustrated. 6 Add a 2 in. wide dart from centre front and side seam to also meet at the bust point.

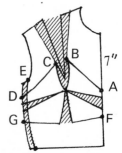

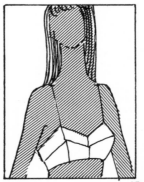

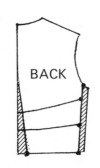

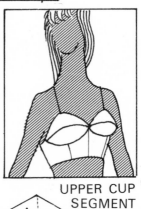

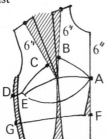

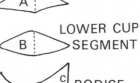

UPPER CUP SEGMENT

LOWER CUP SEGMENT

BODICE FRONT

Brassiere 2

1 Mark A 6 in. down from front neck, and B and C 6 in. down from shoulder. 2 Connect A to B with a convex curved line. 3 Mark D 3 in. down from under arm, and rule a line from D to the bust point. 4 Mark E on this line, 2 in. away from D. 5 Connect C to E with a convex curve. 6 Mark F 3½ in. up from waist line, and G 2 in. up, and connect forming base of brassiere. 7 Move waist dart to under bust, and lengthen to join at the bust point. 8 Draw in lower cup segment as illustrated. 9 Shape centre front seam in 1 in. at base. 10 Cut out bra, and divide segments into upper and lower cup. 11 Close dart in upper cup segment for final pattern.

Brassiere 3

1 Move waist dart to join up with shoulder dart. 2 Draw in style lines of bra making A 6 in. down from neck, and B and C 5 in. down from shoulder. 3 Draw in lower cup as a semicircle ending ¾ in. in from A. 4 Draw in centre seam across cup, passing through the bust point as illustrated. 5 Cut out, and cut away cup portions. 6 Mark the 2 lower cup sections B and C. Close the dart in the top segment, and mark this A. 7 Close the dart in section D and take in 1 in. in centre front at E.

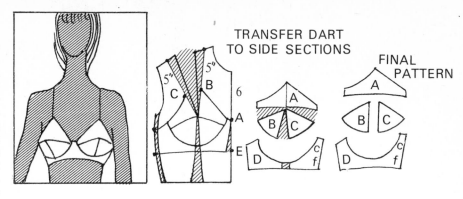

TRANSFER DART TO SIDE SECTIONS

FINAL PATTERN

CAMINICKS

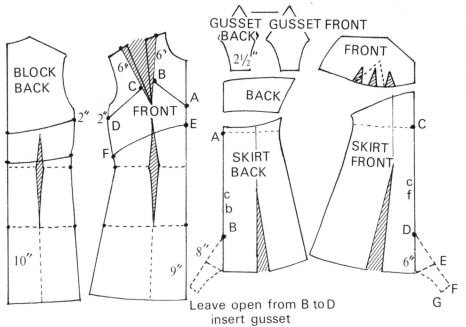

BLOCK BACK

FRONT

GUSSET BACK GUSSET FRONT

FRONT

BACK

SKIRT BACK

SKIRT FRONT

Leave open from B to D insert gusset

Camiknickers

1 Draw round lingerie block lengthening 15 in. below waist in front and 16 in. at the back.

2 Draw in style lines making A 6 in. down from neck and B and C 6 in. down from the shoulder. Mark point D 2 in. below armhole.

3 The skirt section rises to just below the bust, mark E 2½ in. below A, and F 5 in. below D. Connect E to F with a curved line.

4 Cut out, and separate the skirt from the bra.

5 Transfer the shoulder dart to underneath the bust point forming 1 big dart. Divide this into 3 small darts as illustrated.

6 Flare the back and front skirt sections by closing the waist dart and slashing from the hem line up to the point of the dart. Re-draw for final pattern.

7 For gusset inset, mark points B and D 6 in. up from the hem line.

8 To construct gusset, lay a set square to connect up D and E to the hem with a right angle. D to E should measure 4 in. and D to F 8 in. Square out F to G 1¼ in. then connect G to hem at centre front with a curved line.

9 Repeat the same for back gusset.

French knicker draft

1 Draw line AB length required about 16 in. 2 Square out A to D ¼ of waist measurement. 3 Mark point C 7½ in. down from waist level. 4 Square out C to E ¼ hip measurement minus ¼ in. 5 Draw D through E to F forming side seam. D to F equals A to B. 6 Raise G ¾ in. above D and draw front waist line from G to A. 7 To construct crutch, mark point H 1 in. forward from B and connect with straight line to C. This slightly flares the knicker leg. 8 Mark crutch length J 13½ in. (⅓ hip measurement plus 1 in. ease). 9 Square out J to K 3¼ in. ($\frac{1}{12}$ hip measurement). 10 J to L is half the distance from J to K. 11 Curve K through L to C to complete front leg.

FRENCH KNICKER

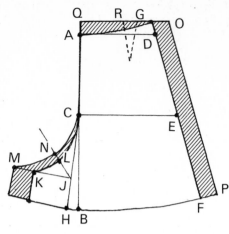

Back leg Extend K to M 2 in. L to N is 1½ in. Join MNC with a curve as illustrated. Square down from M and complete hem of knicker leg. For waist, extend A to Q ¾ in. and D to O 1½ in. Connect O to P with a line parallel to DF. Then connect F to P. At R which is midway between O and Q in the back waist a 1½ in. wide dart may be added. The shaded part of the draft represents the back leg.

Pyjama draft

Pyjama draft The flounced top can be adapted from the bodice block.

1 Extend bodice block to required length, about midway between hip and knee. 2 Straighten side seam and close shoulder dart. 3 Cut out and slash from hem up to point of dart to flare. 4 Lower neck 3 in. and widen armhole as illustrated. 5 Draw in flounce 3 in. deep at the hem, and 1¾ in. deep at the neck. 6 Trace through neck flounce on to fresh paper, cut out and snip and flare to semicircle as illustrated. 7 Cut away hem flounce, and flare in the same way.

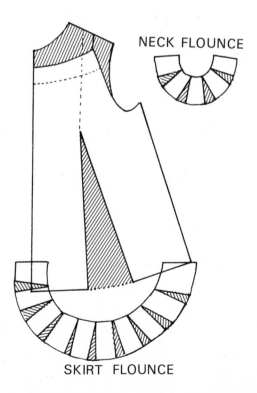

NECK FLOUNCE

SKIRT FLOUNCE

Pyjama trousers This is the usual trouser draft, but ending just above the knee. Two flared flounces are stitched on the lines indicated in the draft.

1 Rule line AB the required length. 2 Square out A to C $\frac{1}{4}$ waist measurement. At D $7\frac{1}{2}$ in. below the waist, square out to L $\frac{1}{4}$ hip measurement minus $\frac{1}{4}$ in. Square down from L to N and connect N to B. 3 At point C measure upwards $\frac{3}{4}$ in. to M, then connect to A with a curved line. 4 For crutch depth, mark point E $13\frac{1}{2}$ in. from A. 5 To construct fork, square out $3\frac{3}{4}$ in. from E to F ($\frac{1}{12}$ hip measurement plus $\frac{1}{2}$ in.). E to G is $\frac{1}{2}$ length of EF. Curve front fork from F through G and D to A. 6 Point K is $\frac{2}{3}$ distance between E and F from B. Connect F to K forming front inside leg seam.

Back leg Extend F to O 2 in. and K to Q $1\frac{1}{2}$ in. Connect O to Q. Point R is midway between E and F and point S is $1\frac{1}{4}$ in. from A. G to U is $\frac{3}{4}$ in. Draw construction line from R through G to S and continuing on $1\frac{1}{4}$ in. to T. Complete back seam by joining *oust*. For back waist line make T to V $\frac{1}{4}$ waist measurement plus 1 in. Draw in waist line. L to W is $1\frac{1}{2}$ in. Square down from W to complete leg.

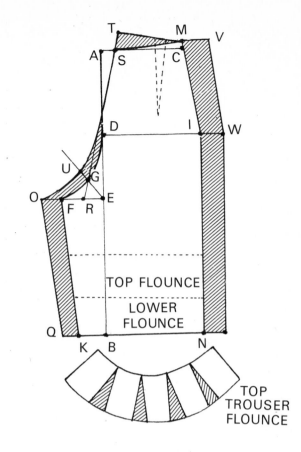

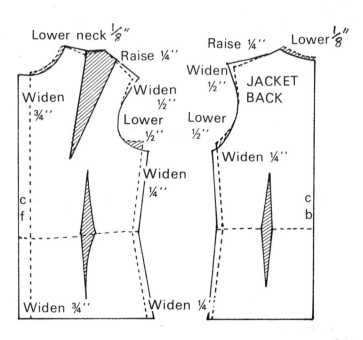

Adapting the bodice block for jacket and costume foundations

So far, the blocks have been used to cut patterns which are intended for use over normal undergarments. In order to cut patterns for jackets and top coats, certain modifications must be made to the blocks; though this can be done when making construction patterns, it is usually quicker to make and keep a set of blocks for this purpose.

The fitted jacket

1 Draw round normal bodice block. 2 Add $\frac{1}{4}$ in. on side seams and on top of shoulder, tapering to nothing at the neck point. 3 Lower armhole $\frac{1}{2}$ in. and widen shoulder point $\frac{1}{2}$ in. graduating into armhole as illustrated. 4 Add $\frac{3}{4}$ in. down centre front. 5 Lower neck $\frac{1}{8}$ in. all round.

Sleeve The sleeve should be widened a total of 1 in., e.g. $\frac{1}{4}$ in. on each underarm seam, $\frac{1}{2}$ in. is added to the top of the crown, also the sleeve is widened $\frac{1}{2}$ in. on the top line. It is best to adapt the sleeve in 2 distinct operations. 1 Widen sleeve seams $\frac{1}{4}$ in. Raise centre of crown $\frac{1}{2}$ in. and lower armhole $\frac{1}{2}$ in. Re-draw new crown line. 2 The sleeve must now be widened $\frac{1}{2}$ in. on the top line. Cut out the sleeve, then cut up the top line and spread open $\frac{1}{2}$ in. as illustrated. Re-draw for final pattern.

Addition for shoulder pads The basic bodice block follows the natural line of the shoulder; if pads are to be inserted, it is necessary to add the required amount on top of the shoulder point. Pads are seldom less than $\frac{1}{4}$–$\frac{1}{2}$ in. thick at the shoulder end; this amount should be added on to both back and front shoulders as illustrated. The crown of the sleeve will also have to be raised the corresponding amount.

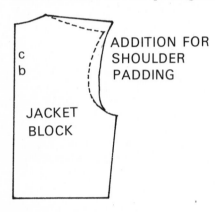

ADDITION FOR SHOULDER PADDING

JACKET BLOCK

Alternative method

Fitted costume foundation For the fitted costume block, the shoulder dart may be brought closer to the neck point, and shortened a little as illustrated. Additional width is added mainly to the front block, whilst the darts in the back block are so arranged as to form a panel seam.

Front

1 Extend centre front $1\frac{3}{4}$ in. 2 Extend side seam $\frac{1}{2}$ in. 3 Widen shoulder point $\frac{1}{2}$ in. and raise $\frac{1}{2}$ in. 4 Lower armhole $\frac{1}{2}$ in. 5 Take $\frac{1}{8}$ in. off neck all round. 6 Lengthen jacket to 10 in. below waist and drop hem in centre front 1 in. Graduate this to nothing at the side seam as illustrated.

Back Adjust armhole and shoulder as in front block, then arrange waist and shoulder darts to form a panel seam.

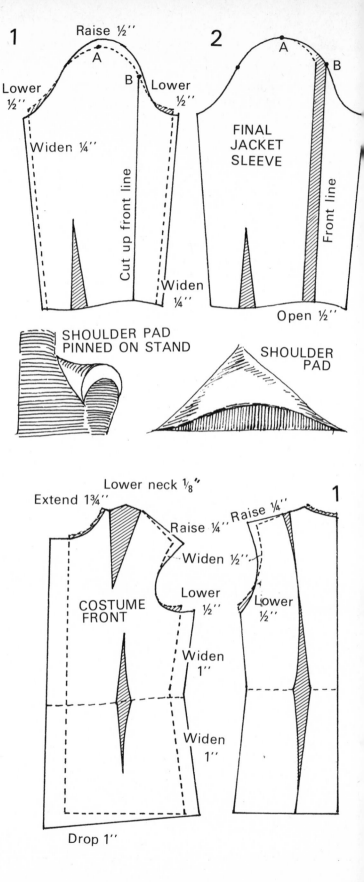

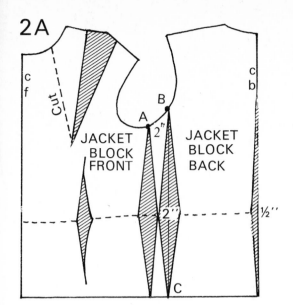

2A

JACKET BLOCK FRONT

JACKET BLOCK BACK

2B

FINAL JACKET FRONT

FINAL JACKET BACK

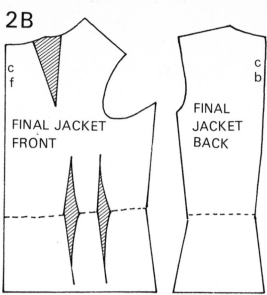

Diagram 2 Frequently coats have the shoulder dart moved into the neck gorge; this is more suitable for certain styles such as the raglan sleeve. Many costume jackets have the side seam place 2 in. towards the centre back giving a more slimming effect. To do this, place the front and back jacket blocks together joining at side seams. Measure 2 in. from A to B and drop a vertical line. Measure 1 in. each side of this line at waist level to form a 2 in. wide dart. Connect point of dart to B as illustrated. The line BC now forms the new side seam to jacket front, whilst the outer line of the dart forms the side seam of the back. The centre back seam may be hollowed at the waist if desired.

Adaptation for coat block The coat block is obtained in exactly the same method as the jacket block, but with a few more modifications.

1 Widen side seams $\frac{1}{2}$ in. 2 Lower armhole 1 in. 3 Raise shoulder point $\frac{1}{4}$ in. graduating to nothing at the neck point. 4 Widen shoulder $\frac{1}{2}$ in. 5 For single breasted style, add 1 in. down centre front, for double breasted style add $3\frac{1}{2}$ in. 7 Lower neck gorge $\frac{1}{4}$ in. all round.

For the current fashion for semi-fitted and unfitted coats, the side seams may be straightened after you have made the additions to the block by ruling a line from the base of armhole to hip level as illustrated. This will now form the unfitted coat block.

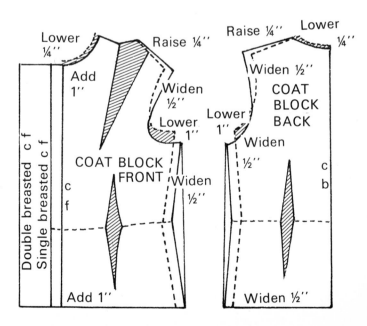

COAT BLOCK FRONT

COAT BLOCK BACK

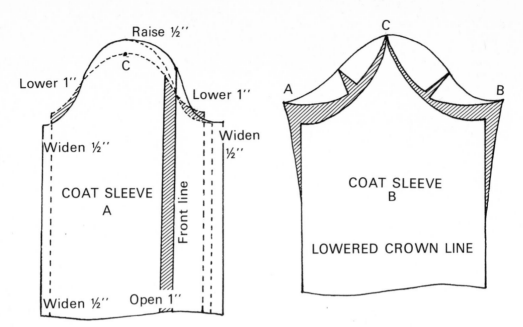

Adaptation for coat sleeve Use the straight sleeve block.
1 Lower armhole 1 in. 2 Widen underarm seams ½ in.
3 Raise crown ½ in. at centre top. 4 Cut out sleeve,
then cut up the front line separating the front portion
from the rest of the sleeve. 5 Lay both sections on to a
clean sheet of paper ½ in. apart as illustrated and re-
draw, adjusting the top of the crown line.

Coat sleeve B With the current fashion for smooth
unpadded shoulders, most coat sleeves are now cut with
a lowered crown line. This can be obtained without
altering the total crown measurement. Proceed by drawing 2 curved lines from A and B under the arms up to C.
Slash along these lines to C and open at A and B 1½ in.
Snip as illustrated across inner line of curve to outer edge
to facilitate maintaining the crown curve. Lay on fresh
paper and re-draw. This will lower the height of the
crown about 1¼ in. whilst still retaining the original
crown measurement.

Car coat Using the coat block
1 Shorten 5 in. 2 Widen under arm ¾ in. and
2 in. at hem level. Draw new side seam.
3 Extend button wrap 1½ in. 4 Drop front
neck 1 in. in centre front. 5 Draw in *raglan
shoulder yoke*, making point F 4 in. down from
shoulder point, and A 1 in. down from neck
point. 6 Add facing to centre front. 7 Place
flap pocket, making it 6 in. wide and 5½ in.
deep. 8 Widen back shoulder dart to ¾ in. by
slashing from side seam along dotted lines and
opening the required amount. 9 Cut away
raglan yokes and close yoke darts as shown in
diagrams F and B. 10 *Raglan sleeve* Draw
round coat sleeve block lowering armhole ½ in.
and widening ¾ in. on underarm seam.
11 Draw centre line up middle of sleeve and
extend to E 1 in. above top of crown. 12 Place
front and back yokes over crown, with shoulder
points each 1 in. away from E as illustrated.
13 Draw round raglan sleeve, raising the
shoulder seams ½ in. at the shoulder point and
meeting in a dart on the centre line. 14 Cut up
centre line to form the sleeve into 2 sections,
front and back.

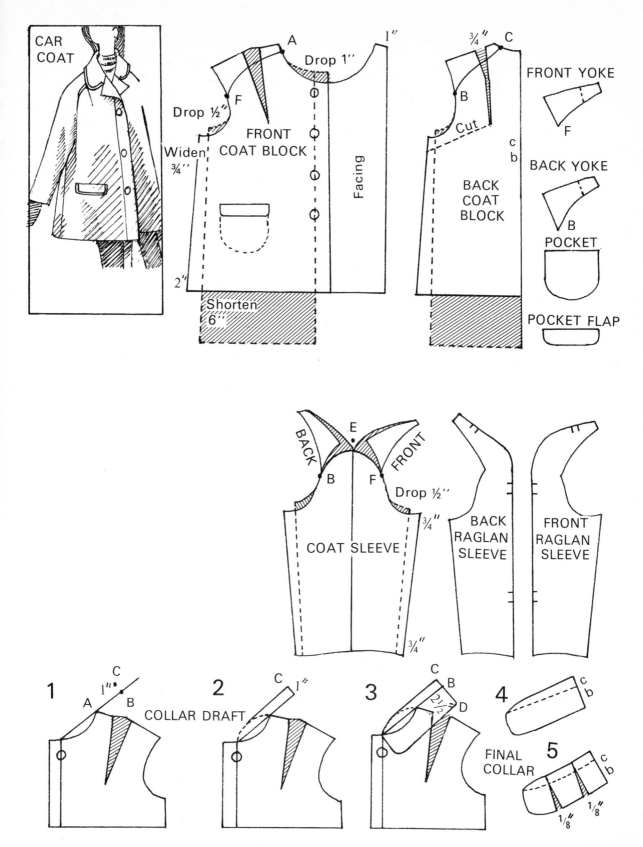

CAR COAT

A Drop 1"

1"

Drop ½" F

FRONT COAT BLOCK

Widen ¾"

Facing

2"

Shorten 6"

¾" C

B

Cut

c b

BACK COAT BLOCK

FRONT YOKE

F

BACK YOKE

B

POCKET

POCKET FLAP

BACK

E

FRONT

B F

Drop ½"

¾"

COAT SLEEVE

¾"

BACK RAGLAN SLEEVE

FRONT RAGLAN SLEEVE

1
C
1"
A B

COLLAR DRAFT

2
C 1"

3
C B
2½
D

4
c b

FINAL COLLAR

5
c b
⅛" ⅛"

Grading patterns to trade sizes

SKIRT BACK
GRADED UP 4 SIZES

SKIRT FRONT
GRADED UP 4 SIZES

Grading is a method of increasing and decreasing a sample size pattern proportionately. The whole system of sizing is based on pattern grading, and every designer should be conversant with it. Size ranges are known in 2 in. increases, such as 32 in., 34 in., 36 in., 38 in., 40 in., or 42 in., these being the actual body measurements round the bust. It is possible to grade in one operation the 6 sizes mentioned, but it is more usual and more accurate today to grade no more than 3 or 4 sizes at a time. As size ranges enlarge at 2 in. intervals, the additional girth measurement on the half pattern is $\frac{1}{2}$ in. The pattern is lengthened $\frac{1}{4}$ in. at shoulder level for each size larger, as also back neck, and both neck and shoulders widen $\frac{1}{8}$ in. for each size increase. The armhole is also widened $\frac{1}{4}$ in. for each size. There are various methods of grading, but the two most commonly used are the shifting method extensively used in the wholesale trade, where the pattern is shifted from point to point to give the required additional measurements, and the method of grading from one pattern only with all the

constructional points marked up on it for each size increase or decrease. This second method is the one used here to illustrate the principle of grading, and it is a method that can be easily checked, and therefore good for the beginner. It is usual in the trade to grade the actual pattern, but for basic illustrative purposes the blocks are here used to explain the principle which can be applied to both lingerie or coat blocks if desired. Commence by grading the skirt blocks, as this is the simplest grade.

Grading the skirt Draw round back and front skirt blocks on a clean sheet of paper. To grade up to 4 sizes larger, add $\frac{1}{2}$ in. for each size up the centre back and front as illustrated. To keep the correct placing of the waist dart, this must also be graded, and it should move forward $\frac{1}{2}$ in. for each size as illustrated. To grade down to size 32 in. take $\frac{1}{2}$ in. off centre back and front; and in this case the waist dart would be moved $\frac{1}{2}$ in. towards the hip. The illustration above shows the 34 in. size skirt block grades up to size 42 in.

Grading the bodice block

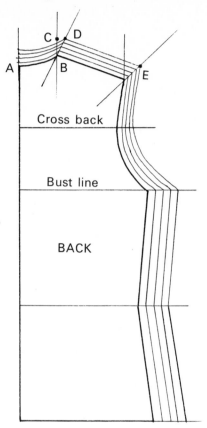

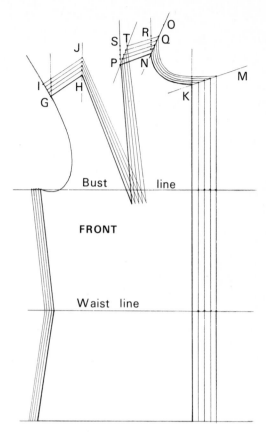

Grading the back bodice

Draw round 34 in. back block. At A extend the back line and mark up 4 points at $\frac{1}{4}$ in. intervals. These represent sizes 34 to 42 in. bust. Rule a vertical line up from B and mark C 1 in. up. At C measure forwards $\frac{1}{2}$ in. to D and connect D to B with a diagonal line. Then divide line DB into 4 equal parts, then connect these points to the centre back neck with grade lines which follow the curve of the neck. Each back neck will now have widened $\frac{1}{4}$ in. From each point on line BD, rule 4 lines parallel to the shoulder line. On the largest size, mark point E $5\frac{1}{2}$ in. from D. This being the shoulder seam length of bust size 42 in. Connect E to original shoulder tip. Continue all shoulder lines to join this line. Extend the across back line and mark outward 4 points at $\frac{1}{4}$ in. intervals, then extend bust and waist lines and mark out at $\frac{1}{2}$ in. intervals on both these lines, as also on the hip line. Grade up the side seam connecting these points, then grade round the back armhole joining the shoulder grade on diagonal line E as illustrated. You now have the completed grades of 4 sizes from bust 34 in. to 42 in.

Grading the front bodice

When grading the front bodice, $\frac{3}{8}$ in. is added up the centre front, and $\frac{1}{8}$ in. is added on to the sideseam. There is no grading round the armhole.

1 Extend bust and waist and hip lines and mark out-

wards four points at $\frac{3}{8}$ in. intervals. Draw the front grade through these points from hip to neckline. Draw the grade on the sideseams at $\frac{1}{8}$ in. intervals as illustrated.

2 The shoulder lengthens $\frac{1}{8}$ in. and rises $\frac{1}{4}$ in. for each size increase. Rule a vertical line upwards from N. Repeat this at P, H and G then mark off points at $\frac{1}{4}$ in. intervals up these lines. At N measure forward $\frac{1}{8}$ in. from the first point, then rule a diagonal line from N passing through this point to O. This gives the angle for the shoulder increase. Repeat this at P making line PT parallel to line NO. To obtain shoulder grades, square-out at right angles from each point on line NR and PS; where these touch the diagonal line will give the correct positioning for each shoulder. Rule in the shoulder grades. Extend the shoulder point from G to I then rule in the shoulder grades from line HJ to line GI.

3 The neck grade rises $\frac{1}{8}$ in. and extends outwards $\frac{3}{8}$ in. on the centre front. Rule a vertical line upwards at K, then measure up at $\frac{1}{8}$ in. intervals. Square forward $\frac{3}{8}$ in. at each point, and where these coincide with the front grade will be the centre front neck as shown in line KM. Draw in the four neck curves parallel to original neckline to meet the shoulders on line NO.

4 The point of the bust dart moves forward $\frac{1}{4}$ in. for each size. Connect to relative shoulder lines.

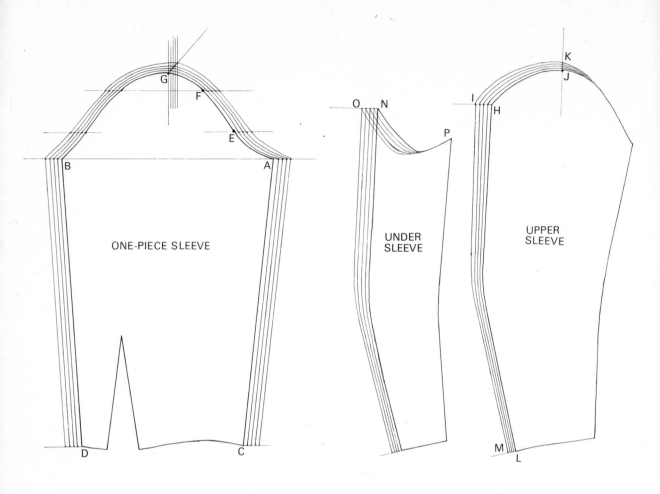

Grading the one-piece and two-piece sleeves

The basis of sleeve grading is the armhole of the pattern, and the measurements obtained from it show an increase of $\frac{1}{2}$ in. through the width of the sleeve, at the base of the armhole, and $\frac{1}{4}$ in. through the sleeve head or crown at point G.

Grading the one-piece sleeve

To grade the sleeve up to 42 in. size, draft out a 34 in. size sleeve, and continue the centre line through the centre of the crown. Extend the bust level line through the base of the armhole at A and B. Add $\frac{1}{4}$ in. at A for each size, and add a similar quantity at B. On the front curve, add $\frac{1}{4}$ in. at point E. Measure 2 in. down from G and rule a line across the top of the sleeve head, where this crosses the front armhole mark this point F. At F extend $\frac{1}{4}$ in. for each size. At G mark forwards $\frac{3}{16}$ in. for each size, and raise crown height a similar quantity in a diagonal line as illustrated. Draw grade line, grading to $\frac{1}{4}$ in. at the back of the crown. At the cuff add equally front and back $\frac{1}{8}$ in. for each size larger.

Grading the two-piece sleeve

1 *The outer sleeve* Draw a short horizontal line H to I through the top of the hind arm seam, and a short vertical line JK through the centre of the crown. Mark outwards on line HI $\frac{1}{4}$ in. for each size larger, then measure up from J $\frac{1}{8}$ in. for each size, and mark outwards at L $\frac{1}{8}$ in. on the wrist. Draw in the grade lines as illustrated.

2 *The under sleeve grade* The under sleeve is graded in a similar way. Draw a short horizontal line NO through the top of the hind arm, and mark outwards $\frac{1}{4}$ in. for each size larger, and $\frac{1}{8}$ in. for each size at the wrist. Draw in the grade lines as shown. The front of the under sleeve is not graded, and the grading on the sleeve base should be graduated to P as shown in the diagram.

To grade down a size smaller, mark corresponding measurements inwards along the measuring lines. This ensures keeping the grading proportional.

Check your sleeve measurements with the graded bodices, remembering that in every case the ease on the sleeve makes it measure 2 in. more than the armhole.

Drafting children's clothes

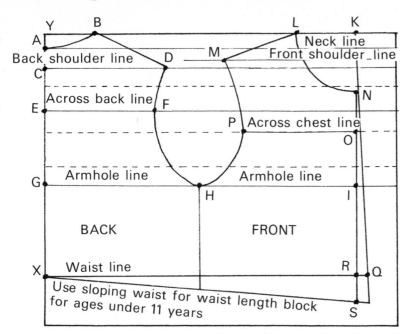

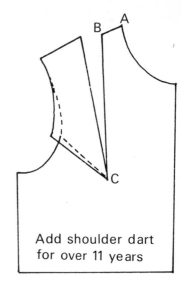

Add shoulder dart for over 11 years

Child's bodice block

When the age of the child is known, use the following proportions.

Height	For 3 years equals 3 ft 1 in. Add 2 in. for each year up to 10 years.
Bust	Up to 5 years measure 20 in. plus age—1 in. After 5 years measure 20 in. plus age—2 in.
Length to waist	One quarter of height
Length of dress	One half of height
Across back	One quarter of height. In larger sizes one quarter of height minus $\frac{1}{2}$ in.
Across chest	One quarter of height
Shoulder length	One third across back

If possible, work from individual measurements.

Drafting the block Take a rectangular piece of paper of the following dimensions

Length = Length to waist plus 2 in.
Width = Half bust plus 3 in.

Draft the block, using the above diagram in conjunction with the instructions:

Rule *neck line* $\frac{1}{2}$ in. below top of paper.
A to X = length from neck to waist. Rule *waist line*.
Fold waist line to neck line, and rule a line $\frac{1}{2}$ in. below the crease. Mark this *armhole line*.
Fold armhole line to neck line, and mark crease line *across back line*.
Fold across back line to neck line and rule a line $\frac{1}{2}$ in.

above crease line and mark this *back shoulder line*.
Y to B is width of back neck ($\frac{1}{12}$ of bust measure). Draw neck curve AB.
B to D = shoulder length ($\frac{1}{3}$ of *across back*) plus $\frac{1}{4}$ in. Measure this length from B to meet back shoulder line.
G to H = $\frac{1}{2}$ *across back* plus $1\frac{3}{4}$ in. Draw armhole curve DFH. Rule side seam parallel to centre back line.
Y to K = $\frac{1}{2}$ bust measure plus 2 in. Square out KS. This is the centre front line parallel to centre back line.
K to L = back neck width. *Front neck line* is drawn in a square of this measure, so K to N equals K to L.
Draw *front shoulder line* $\frac{1}{4}$ in. above shoulder line used for the back.
L to M = *shoulder length*, $\frac{1}{3}$ across back measure. Measure from point L to meet front shoulder line.
Across chest is midway between the pit of the neck and armhole; obtain this by folding N to I.
O to P = $\frac{1}{2}$ *across chest*. Draw armhole curve MPH.
The centre front line may be sloped out by marking Q $\frac{1}{2}$ in. from R on the *waist line*, and ruling N to Q.
A *sloping waist line* for waist length blocks, is obtained by making R to S 1 in. for ages 2–4 years; $\frac{3}{4}$ in. for ages 5–7 years and $\frac{1}{2}$ in. for ages 8–10 years. Ages 11–13 years do not require a sloping waist at all. In these larger sizes a dart from shoulder to bust may be necessary. To make a dart, mark point B 1 in. away from A, and rule a dart line to C, which is on the armhole line and 2 in. in from centre front. Slash along this line and open to give a dart about $\frac{1}{2}$ in. wide on the shoulder. This can vary according to individual development. Flatten out the pattern by folding a small dart into the armhole curve below the chest line. Stick this down, and adjust the armhole curve as shown.

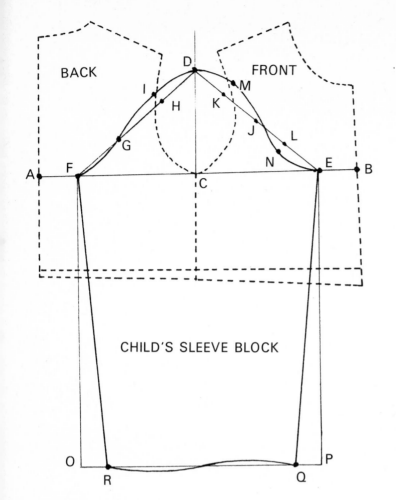

BACK   FRONT

CHILD'S SLEEVE BLOCK

Child's sleeve draft

1 Lay child's bodice blocks together, joining along side seam. 2 Rule a line from A to B passing through C. 3 Rule a line vertically up from C to D. 4 Point D is $\frac{1}{3}$ of the total armhole measure. Measure this length up from C. 5 To locate point E, take the front armhole measure plus $\frac{1}{4}$ in. for ease, and measure this from point D. Where this measure strikes line CB will be point E. 6 Locate point F in the same way by measuring the back armhole and adding $\frac{1}{4}$ in. ease. 7 For back crown construction, divide line FD into 3 equal parts. Mark division spots G and H. 8 To obtain back curve, measure out $\frac{1}{4}$ in. from H to I, then connect D to F with a curved line passing through I and G to F as illustrated. 9 For front crown, divide line DE into half and mark this point J, then subdivide J to D in half at point K, and J to E in half at L. 10 To obtain front curve, at point K measure outwards $\frac{1}{2}$ in. to M, and at L measure inwards $\frac{1}{4}$ in. to N. Connect D to E passing through M and N to E as illustrated. The curve of the crown line will cross over line DE about $\frac{1}{4}$ in. away from point J. This is correct. 11 Square down from F to O and E to P making this the full-length sleeve. 12 At O and P measure in $\frac{3}{4}$ in. for wrist measure. 13 Draw in wrist curve as illustrated. It should drop $\frac{1}{8}$ in. below line OP at the back, and rise $\frac{1}{8}$ in. above this line in the front.

CHILD'S KNICKER DRAFT

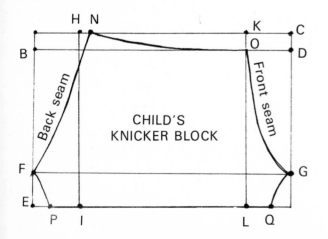

CHILD'S KNICKER BLOCK

Back seam

Front seam

Child's knicker block draft

When only the age of the child is known, the following average measures may be used:

Loose hips = Bust measure plus 2 in.
Waist size 1 = Bust measure
        Age 2–4 years
    size 2 = Bust minus 1 in.
        Age 5–7 years
    size 3 = Bust minus 2 in.
        Age 8–10 years
    size 4 = Bust minus 3 in.
        Age 11–14 years
Leg width for girls = $\frac{3}{4}$ loose hip
Leg width for boys = $\frac{3}{4}$ loose hip minus 1 in.
Crutch length = $\frac{1}{4}$ height.

If possible, work from individual measurements.

Drafting the block Take a rectangular sheet of paper of the following dimensions

Length = Crutch depth plus $4\frac{3}{4}$ in.
Width = Leg width
AB = $1\frac{3}{4}$ in. Draw line BD parallel to AC.
EF = $3\frac{1}{2}$ in. Draw line FG parallel to AC.
AH = 3 in. Draw line HI parallel to AE.
CK = $2\frac{1}{2}$ in. Draw line KL parallel to AE.
Draw line from F through M to meet top edge of paper.
Mark point N. Line FN is the centre back line.
Draw line NO (waist line) and O to G (centre front line) as illustrated.

IP = $1\frac{3}{4}$ in. Connect to FP with a curved line (leg seam line).
LQ = $1\frac{1}{2}$ in. Draw line GQ (front leg seam line).

Children's skirts

No skirt block is used, but a *dress block* can be obtained by prolonging the side seam and centre front and back lines to the required length. Skirts are usually straight pieces of material, either pleated or gathered. If it is flared base the skirt on the child's dress block, and cut and flare it in the usual way.

INFANT'S BLOCK LENGTHENED INTO FULL-LENGTH DRESS BLOCK

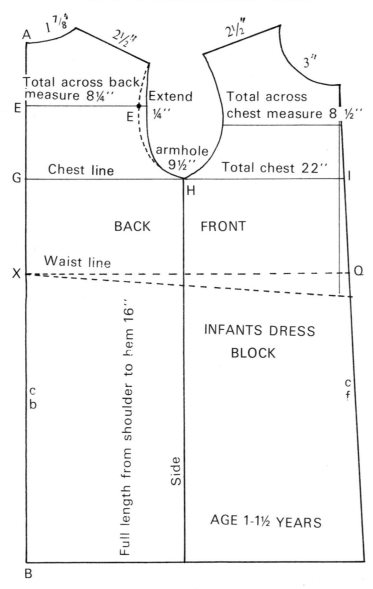

Children's body measurements

Age (*approx.*)	1½	2	3	3½	4	5	6	7	8
Weight	st. lb.	st. lb.	st. lb.	st. lb.	st. lb.	st. lb.	st. lb.	st. lb.	st. lb.
	1 11	2 0	2 4	2 10	3 0	3 4	3 8	4 0	4 8
	(25 lb.)	(28 lb.)	(32 lb.)	(38 lb.)	(42 lb.)	(46 lb.)	(50 lb.)	(56 lb.)	(64 lb.)
Stature	ft. in.	ft. in.	ft. in.	ft. in.	ft. in.	ft. in.	ft. in.	ft. in.	ft. in.
	2 7½	2 10	3 1	3 4½	3 7	3 9	3 11½	4 2	4 4
	(31½ in.)	(34 in.)	(37 in.)	(40½ in.)	(43 in.)	(45 in.)	(47½ in.)	(50 in.)	(52 in.)
Girth	in.	in.	in.	in.	in.	in.	in.	in.	in.
Chest	19¼	20¼	21¼	22	22½	23¼	24	24⅞	26
Waist	19	19½	19¾	20	20¼	20⅝	21	21⅝	22½
Hip	20	20¾	21¾	22½	23⅜	24⅛	25	26⅛	27⅝
Vertical-trunk	30½	32½	34½	37¼	38¾	40	41½	43	45
Neck-base	9⅝	10	10⅜	10¾	11	11¼	11½	11⅞	12⅛
Armscye	8½	9	9½	10	10¼	10⅝	10⅞	11⅜	11⅞
Thigh	11½	12	12½	13⅛	13½	14	14⅜	15⅛	16⅛
Height									
(*measured over body*)									
Cervical to waist	8	8½	9	9¾	9¾	10⅛	10⅝	11	11⅜
Waist to hip	3½	4	4½	5¼	5½	5¾	6	6⅜	6⅝
Width									
Cross back	8⅜	8⅞	9¼	9½	9¾	10⅛	10½	10⅞	11¼
Length									
Total crutch	15	16	17	17¾	18½	19¼	20	21	22
Shoulder	—	—	—	2⅞	3	3⅛	3¼	3½	3⅝
Posterior arm	—	—	—	14⅛	15	15⅞	16¾	17¾	18⅝
Combined shoulder and posterior arm	12½	13¾	15	—	—	—	—	—	—

The above extracts from *B.S. 1662, 1952 Light Outerwear for Infants and Girls* are reproduced by permission of
The British Standards Institution,
2 Park Street, London, W.1
from whom copies of the complete standard may be obtained.

Toddler's rompers Cutting rompers is very similar to cutting a dress, therefore use the child's dress block to cut this pattern.

Front

1 Draw round the front dress block. 2 Draw in shoulder yoke, making the shoulder seam 3½ in. wide, and 2¾ in. deep in the centre front. 3 Drop armhole ½ in. 4 Widen the hem line ¾ in. at the side seam, and mark point E. Draw in new side seam. 5 The centre front line must be lengthened to pass under the crutch, so mark B ¾ in. from A, then mark C 1½ in. from A and drop down 1½ in. to D. Connect D to B with a curved line. 6 Cut out the draft, and cut away yoke. 7 Slash up the centre of the pattern along the dotted line, and spread open 2 in. 9 Place over fresh paper and re-draw, making D to E a curved line. This is the romper leg opening, which will have elastic inserted.

Back

The back is constructed in the same way as the front, but the extension for under the crutch is longer. Make F to G 2¼ in.; square out from F to H 1½ in. then measure 3¼ in. from H down to I. Cut out draft, then cut away back yoke. Cut up the dotted line and spread open at hem about 3 in. Lay over fresh paper and re-draw putting in button extension from point J; make this 1¼ in. wide. Point J should be about 6 in. up from the hem. Now check your pattern; the back should be about 2 in. longer than the front. The front and back crutch curves should measure the same. This will be left open and fastened with poppers.

9	10/11	12	13	14/15
st. lb.	st. lb.	st. lb.	st. lb.	st. lb.
5 3	5 13	6 11	7 9	8 6
(73 lb.)	(83 lb.)	(95 lb.)	(107 lb.)	(118 lb.)
ft. in.	ft. in.	ft. in.	ft. in.	ft. in.
4 6½	4 9	4 11½	5 1½	5 4
(54½ in.)	(57 in.)	(59½ in.)	(61½ in.)	(64 in.)
in.	in.	in.	in.	in.
27¼	28⅝	30½	32⅛	33¼
23⅜	24⅛	24⅝	25⅛	25⅝
29⅛	30¾	32¾	34¾	36¼
47⅛	49¾	52	54⅜	56½
12½	13	13½	14	14⅜
12½	13⅛	13¾	14⅜	14⅞
17⅛	18	19	20⅛	21⅛
11⅞	12⅜	13¼	14	14⅜
7	7⅜	7¾	8⅛	8½
11⅝	12⅛	12⅝	13	13⅜
23	24¼	25½	26¾	27¾
3¾	4	4⅛	4¼	4⅜
19⅝	20⅝	21⅝	22½	23⅜
—	—	—	—	—

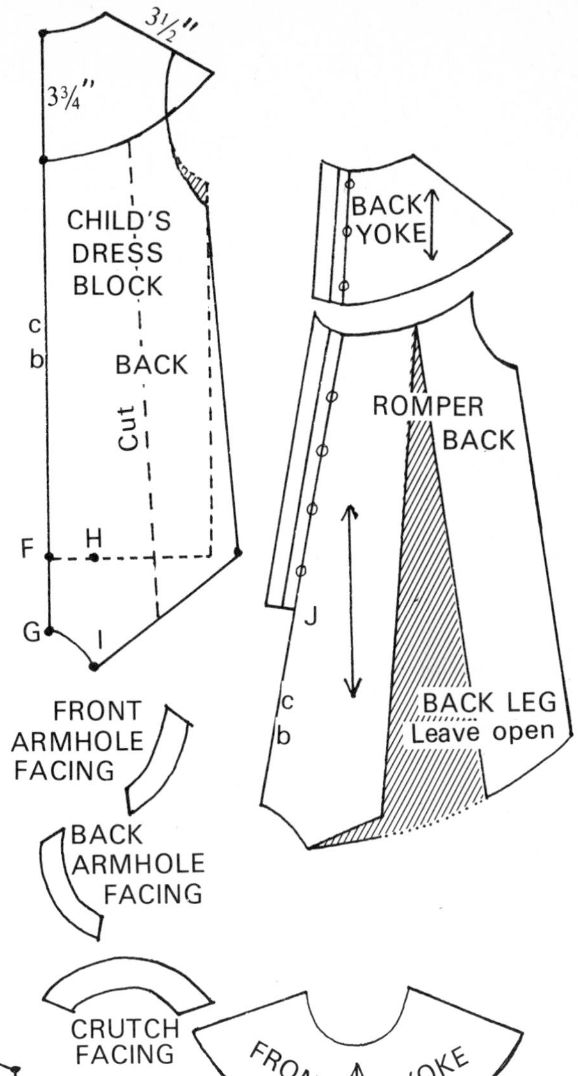
3½"
3¾"
CHILD'S DRESS BLOCK
BACK
Cut
c
b
F
H
G
I
BACK YOKE
ROMPER BACK
J
c
b
BACK LEG
Leave open
FRONT ARMHOLE FACING
BACK ARMHOLE FACING
CRUTCH FACING

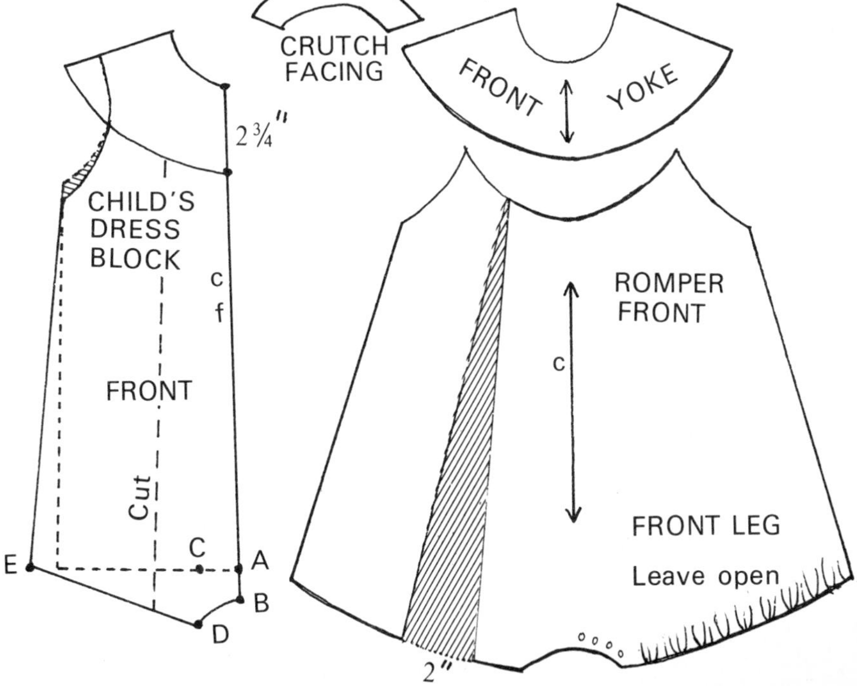
2¾"
CHILD'S DRESS BLOCK
c
f
FRONT
Cut
E
C
A
B
D
FRONT YOKE
ROMPER FRONT
c
FRONT LEG
Leave open
2"

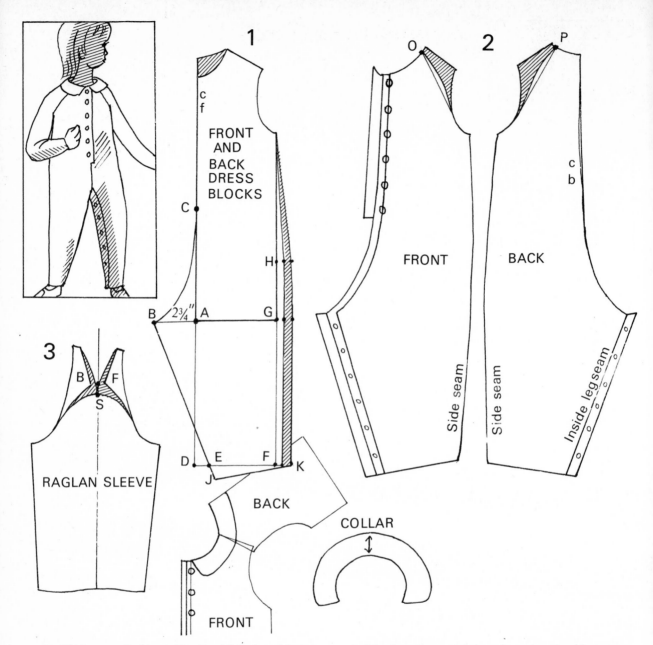

1 FRONT AND BACK DRESS BLOCKS

2 FRONT BACK

3 RAGLAN SLEEVE

BACK

FRONT

COLLAR

Toddler's coverall playsuit Use the child's dress block to construct this draft. This style has raglan sleeves, buttons down centre front, and is fastened with poppers along both inside leg seams.

1 Place dress blocks together, front over back as illustrated. 2 Extend A to D 9 in. 3 To construct fork, mark point C 7 in. up from A then square out A to B 2¾ in. 4 Connect B to C with a curve as illustrated. 5 ½ in. ease is added at F, G and H. Draw in side seam through these points. 6 The back must be widened even more, by adding a further ¾ in. at F and ½ in. at H; draw in back side seam. 7 To construct ankle, mark point E 2 in. in from D. Rule a line from B to E and continue on 2 in. more to J forming the inside leg seam. 8 Connect J to K to complete leg. 9 Trace off separate front and back patterns and draw in raglan shoulder seams, making point O and P ½ in. from the neck point. 10 Add ¾ in. button extension down centre front, and continue this down inside leg seam for poppers. 11 In front section only add facing to popper extension and down centre front to point C. 12 Cut away raglan shoulder yokes and place over crown of sleeve as illustrated. Point R should be ½ in. up from S and the 2 shoulder points should be placed ½ in. each side of R as shown in the diagram. Draw in new shoulder seams meeting at R forming a dart. The raglan sleeve is now complete. Draft the collar as a flat collar by laying the blocks together overlapping the shoulder seams ½ in. at the shoulder tips.

TODDLERS SMOCK AND KNICKERS

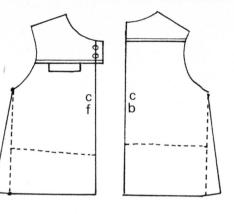

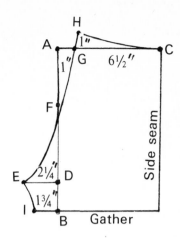

Toddler's smock and knickers
Knicker draft These are gathered both at the waist and leg.
1 Rule line from A to B 10 in. long. 2 Square out A to C ¼ waist measurement plus 1 in. ease = 6½ in. 3 Mark crutch depth D 8 in. from A. 4 Square out D to E 2¼ in. and B to I 1¾ in. Rule bottom of leg. 5 To obtain crutch curve for front leg, mark point F 7 in. up from D. Connect E to F continuing on to A for front seam.
Back leg Mark point G 1 in. from A and connect E to G with a curve as illustrated, continuing on 1 in. above to H. Connect H to C as shown for back waist line.

Play overalls First, draft out the 3-year-old's bodice block.
1 Lay blocks together joining at C as illustrated. 2 Make A to B 29 in. 3 Rule in waist line. 4 Mark G 9 in. down from waist. 5 Square out G to I 2¾ in. 6 Mark E 8 in. up from G. 7 Connect I to E with a curved line forming centre front seam. 8 For inside leg seam, mark L ½ in. from B and connect to I with a curved line. 9 For back leg repeat construction same as the front. 10 To complete, draw in ankle line from L to K. This should measure 15 in.
Apron top Mark M 2 in. down from A and square out 2½ in. Then rule a line to N which is 3½ in. from centre front. The top should be made up separately and then joined to the trouser legs

Play overalls

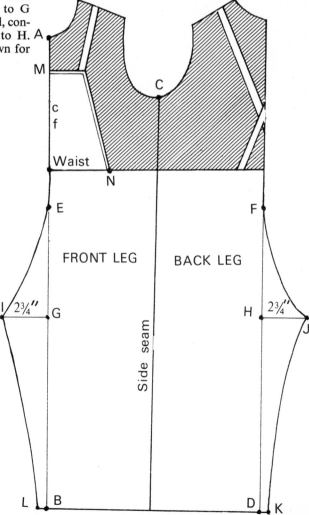

3 YEAR OLD PLAY OVERALLS

after they have been sewn together. The 2 shoulder straps should be 14 in. in length, crossing over at the back as illustrated.

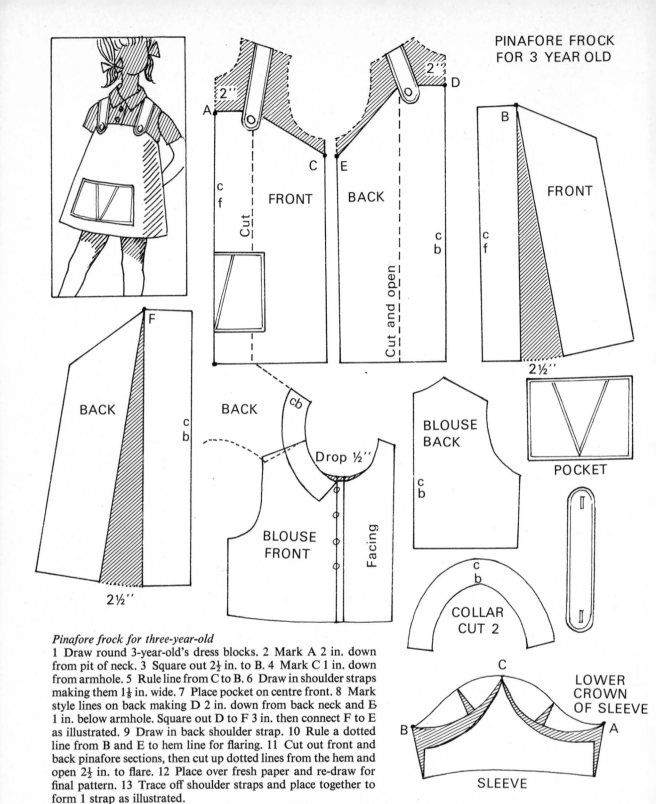

Pinafore frock for three-year-old

1 Draw round 3-year-old's dress blocks. 2 Mark A 2 in. down from pit of neck. 3 Square out $2\frac{1}{2}$ in. to B. 4 Mark C 1 in. down from armhole. 5 Rule line from C to B. 6 Draw in shoulder straps making them $1\frac{1}{2}$ in. wide. 7 Place pocket on centre front. 8 Mark style lines on back making D 2 in. down from back neck and E 1 in. below armhole. Square out D to F 3 in. then connect F to E as illustrated. 9 Draw in back shoulder strap. 10 Rule a dotted line from B and E to hem line for flaring. 11 Cut out front and back pinafore sections, then cut up dotted lines from the hem and open $2\frac{1}{2}$ in. to flare. 12 Place over fresh paper and re-draw for final pattern. 13 Trace off shoulder straps and place together to form 1 strap as illustrated.

The blouse has a flat collar and the crown of the sleeve should be lowered. Do this by drawing curved lines from A and B up to C. Slash along these lines and raise A and B $1\frac{1}{2}$ in. Snip centre of raised sections for easier handling and re-draw.

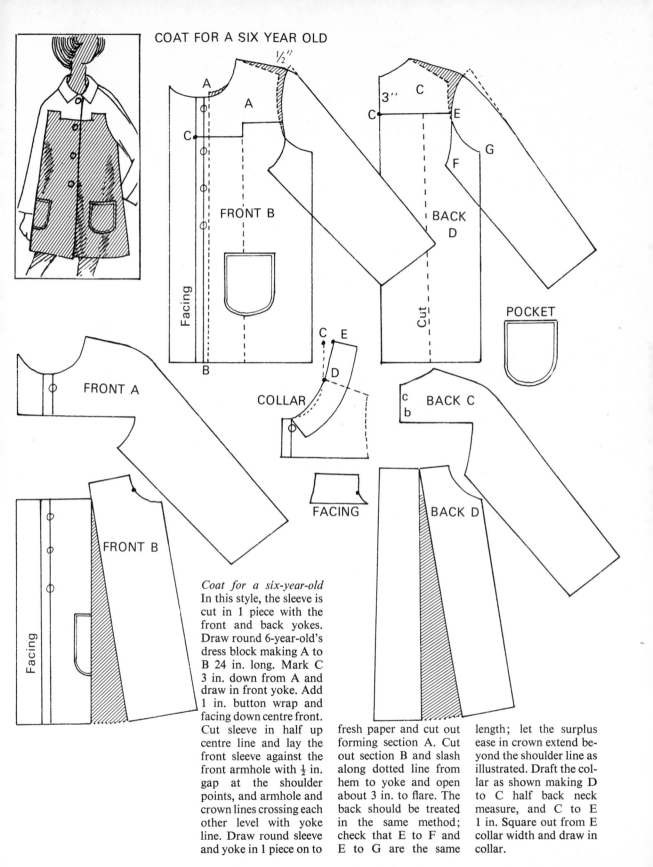

COAT FOR A SIX YEAR OLD

Coat for a six-year-old
In this style, the sleeve is cut in 1 piece with the front and back yokes. Draw round 6-year-old's dress block making A to B 24 in. long. Mark C 3 in. down from A and draw in front yoke. Add 1 in. button wrap and facing down centre front. Cut sleeve in half up centre line and lay the front sleeve against the front armhole with $\frac{1}{2}$ in. gap at the shoulder points, and armhole and crown lines crossing each other level with yoke line. Draw round sleeve and yoke in 1 piece on to

fresh paper and cut out forming section A. Cut out section B and slash along dotted line from hem to yoke and open about 3 in. to flare. The back should be treated in the same method; check that E to F and E to G are the same

length; let the surplus ease in crown extend beyond the shoulder line as illustrated. Draft the collar as shown making D to C half back neck measure, and C to E 1 in. Square out from E collar width and draw in collar.

111

Bibliography

Dress Creation,
Philip H. Richards, Marshall

Dress Design,
Elizabeth Wray, Studio

Your Pattern Cutting,
E. S. MacEwan, Sylvan Home Craft Series

Pattern Drafting and Grading Womens and Misses Garments,
M. Rohr, New York

Dress Design,
Marion S. Hillhouse and A. Mansfield, Houghton, New York

Dressmaking Techniques for Trade Students,
Winifred Clark, Batsford

The Technique of Dress Design
Brenda Naylor, Batsford

Garment-Cutting and Tailoring for Students
Bertha Moulton, Batsford

Introducing Pattern Cutting, Grading and Modelling
Margaritha Goulbourn

British Standard's Publications. *Size Fittings For Women's and Children's Clothing*

Specifications for Lingerie, Women's Blouses and *Light Outer Wear for Infants and Girls*

Equipment and Suppliers

The equipment needed for pattern cutting is very little, but it is important that the student has the correct tools and materials.

Dressmakers drafting paper (*plain*) *36 in. × 46 in.*
This can be bought by the quire or by the ream from MacCulloch and Wallis Ltd, 25/26 Dering Street, London W.1, and from Leighton Baldwin and Cox Ltd, Grovebory Road, Leighton Buzzard, Bedfordshire.

Manilla paper or *thin card* large enough for making foundation blocks.
Obtainable from F. G. Kettle and Co, 127 High Holborn, London W.C.1, or whole rolls can be ordered from E. A. Alexander and Co. Ltd, Patriot Square, Cambridge Heath Road, London E.2.

Yardstick or *dressmaker's square*
$\frac{1}{4}$ *in and* $\frac{1}{8}$ *in. scale dressmaker's square*
Tracing wheel
Pattern notcher (not essential for the beginner)
These can be obtained from Franks Ltd, Kent House, Market Place, London W.1.

Tape measure
Scissors (for cutting paper)
Shears (for cutting cloth)
Dressmaker's steel pins
Dressmaker's mull or *unbleached calico* (for testing out the block pattern)
All these can be obtained from MacCulloch and Wallis Ltd, 25/26 Dering Street, London W.1.

Dressmaker's dummy stand
Obtainable from Siegel and Stockman Ltd, 22 Dering Street, London W.1.